Campus English 103

Campus English 103

English Textbook Committee

SHINGU PUBLISHING CO.

Preface

Welcome to *Campus English 103*, the third book in our textbook series designed for college and university students in Korea. Building on the foundation of *Campus English 101* and *102*, this edition continues to enhance your English skills with engaging lessons that are both practical and relevant to student life.

Like its predecessor, *Campus English 103* has twelve units, each designed for a two-hour class but adaptable for extended sessions with supplementary materials. The textbook follows a consistent format, helping you navigate each unit with ease.

Unit Structure

1. **Warm up:** Start each unit with an interactive activity to spark interest and set the tone for the lesson.

2. **Vocabulary:** Learn key topic-based words essential for effective communication.

3. **Grammar Focus:** Master fundamental grammar concepts for accurate and fluent expression.

4. **Pattern Practice:** Reinforce grammar skills through structured speaking and writing exercises.

5. Dialogue (Listening & Speaking): Improve listening and speaking skills with realistic dialogues.

6. Reading: Strengthen comprehension with texts relevant to university life, supported by audio for pronunciation practice.

7. Conversation Practice: Develop conversational fluency through interactive speaking activities.

8. Editing: Test your grammar and syntax knowledge by identifying and correcting errors.

9. Sentence Scramble: Enhance your grammar, word order, and sentence structure by rearranging mixed-up words to form the correct sentence.

Additional Features

- **Review Units (6 & 12):** Consolidate learning with comprehensive reviews to track progress and prepare for assessments.

- **Workbook:** Gain extra practice with exercises that reinforce each unit's key concepts.

Whether you are an intermediate learner or continuing your English journey, *Campus English 103* is here to support your growth. We hope you find this textbook both enriching and enjoyable as you advance in your studies.

Table of Contents

Unit 01

How's college life going?

Warm up:

Think about your college life so far. In pairs or small groups, ask and answer these questions:

- What is your typical day like in college?
- What do you enjoy most about college life?
- What's one challenging thing about college life?
- How do you balance your studies and free time?

Try to share an interesting answer with the class!

Vocabulary:

Match the words with the correct definition.

1. syllabus ________
2. career fair ________
3. sports festival ________
4. midterms ________
5. final exam ________

6. extracurricular activities ________
7. club fair ________
8. student union ________
9. school cafeteria ________
10. library ________

Definition:

a. a school event focused on sports competitions
b. an exam taken at the end of a semester
c. an outline of a course
d. activities outside regular classes
e. a building on campus where students gather and socialize
f. an event where students join various school clubs
g. a quiet place where students study or read book
h. a place on campus where students buy and eat meals
i. an event where job opportunities are offered to students
j. exams taken in the middle of a semester

Grammar Focus:

Let's learn about asking sentences using the following words. These question words help us gather information.

The question words (5 ***W****s* and ***H***) are:

Who	asks about people.
What	asks about something or someone.
When	asks about time.
Where	asks about place.
Why	asks about reason/cause.
How	asks about function.

Structure #1: When you are asking a question, the verb comes before the subject.

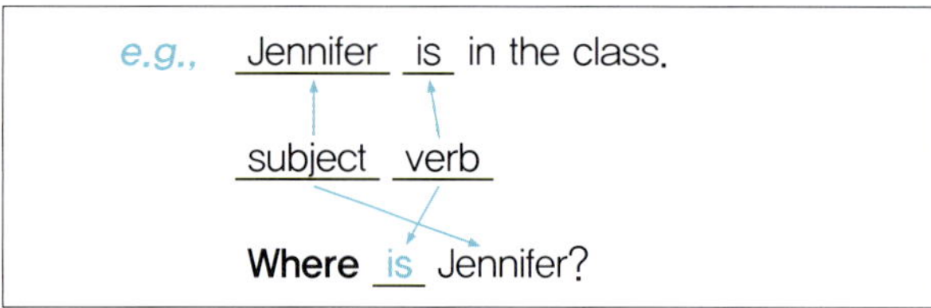

Structure #2: Use helping verbs (such as ***do / does / did*** and ***be*** verb, etc.)

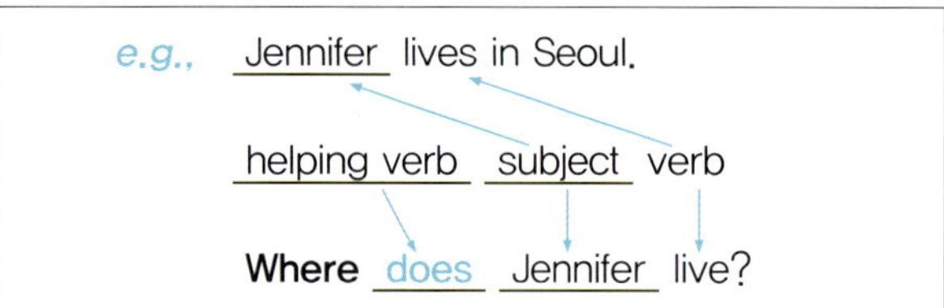

Think of it this way: When forming a question, the helping verb helps the main verb, so the main verb doesn't change. The helping verb comes before the subject.

Let's practice by changing the following statements into questions.

e.g., Tom is going to school.

Who: *Who is going to school?*

Where: *Where is Tom going?*

Pattern Practice:

1. David attended a lecture today. **(who)**

____

2. The lecture was about time management. **(what)**

____

3. The lecture took place in the large classroom. **(where/did)**

____

4. The lecture started at 10 a.m. **(when/did)**

____

5. David attended the lecture to prepare for his exams. **(why/did)**

____

6. He took notes using his laptop. **(how/did)**

____

7. He attended the lecture with his classmates. **(who(m)/did)**

____

Dialogue (Listening and Speaking):

Listen to the dialogue and fill in the missing words. Then practice the dialogue with your partner twice.

Sujin:	Hey, how's college life going for you?
Alex:	So far so good! I joined a few clubs, and that made things more fun. How's it going for you?
Sujin:	Same here. I'm in the photography club. Do you know about the *Baekma* (1)____________________?
Alex:	Oh yeah! I heard that it will be held next month. (2) ________________ sports teams are you playing on?
Sujin:	I'm more into watching. I love the cheerleading competitions. The cheerleading event is one of the best things about it.
Alex:	I agree. Cheerleading is one of the best parts. (3) ___________ don't we watch it together?
Sujin:	Sure! I'm excited for both the Sports Festival and the Shingu Expo. We're preparing a photo **exhibition** for the Expo.

Alex: That sounds great! (4) ______________ is the Shingu Expo?

Sujin: It will take place next **semester**. Our club will display some great photos.

Alex: That's awesome! I'll check it out. (5) _______________ exhibition are you excited about?

Sujin: Probably our club's, but there will be other interesting ones too. (6) _________ in your class will take part in the event?

Alex: Some of my classmates will show their design projects. Events like the Sports Festival and Shingu Expo really make college life fun.

Sujin: Exactly. We can **maintain a balance** between studying and having fun through those school events.

Key words: exhibition 전시회 / semester 학기 / maintain a balance 균형을 유지하다

Reading: Read the passage and answer the questions.

Etiquette in College and Everyday Life

College life is about studying and interacting respectfully with others. Good etiquette creates a positive environment on campus and in daily life.

Hold the door open for the person behind you as a simple act of kindness, whether you're at school, in a cafe, or at a store. Cover your mouth with your elbow or a tissue when coughing or sneezing to prevent the spread of **germs** and show **consideration** for those around you. Keep your voice low in libraries or study areas to avoid **disturbing** others. Respect personal space, as some people prefer to **maintain** distance when talking, whether in class or in a social setting. Use polite expressions like "thank you" and "I'm sorry" to show respect and build good relationships. These simple words can make a big difference in **fostering** positive interactions.

Practicing good etiquette helps create a positive environment and makes life more pleasant for everyone.

Key words: germs 세균 / consideration 고려, 배려 / disturbing 방해하는 / maintain 유지하다 / fostering 촉진하는

Reading Questions: Answer the following questions.

1. Why is holding the door open for someone considered good etiquette?

   ____

2. Why should you cover your mouth when coughing or sneezing?

   ____

3. Where should you keep your voice low to avoid disturbing others?

   ____

4. What are two polite expressions mentioned in the passage?

   ____

5. How does practicing good etiquette benefit everyone?

   ____

Writing and Conversation:

Fill out the card below to introduce yourself. Once yours is complete, ask your partner the questions using the sample question sentences provided below.

You

First Name: ____________________ Last Name: ____________________

English Name: ____________________

Meaning of my name: ____

Mobile phone number: ____

E-mail address: ____

I'm a freshman / sophomore / junior / senior.

(Same as: I'm in my 1st / 2nd / 3rd / 4th year.)

Interests: ____

Things I dislike: ____

Favorite places on campus: ____

Here are some questions you can ask your partner:

1. What is your first name/last name/English name?
2. What does your name mean?
3. Do you have a nickname? If so, what is it?
4. What year are you in university: freshman, sophomore, junior, or senior?
5. What is your mobile phone number or email address?
6. What are your interests and what do you enjoy doing in your free time?
7. Where do you like to hang out or study on campus?

Exercises:

Rearrange the words in each scrambled sentence to form a correct question.

1. in / the photography club / who / is

2. place / the Sports Festival / where / take / does

3. the Shingu Expo / when / take place / will

4. events / campus / enjoy / do / they / how

5. college clubs / join / does / Alex / why

Unit 02

Are you going to enjoy yourself this weekend?

Warm up:

Do you like watching movies and going to the cinema? Think of your favorite movie, but keep it a secret! Act out one or more scenes from the movie without talking. Your classmates will try to guess the movie. The first person to guess correctly gets a turn to act!

Vocabulary:

Match each description to an entertainment-related word.

1. celebrity	_____	a.	a story acted out on stage
2. performance	_____	b.	the sound of people clapping their hands to show praise
3. audience	_____	c.	an event where the public can see art or objects
4. pop culture	_____	d.	a person who guides an orchestra
5. play	_____	e.	a well-known person in the entertainment business
6. theater	_____	f.	a large group of people playing musical instruments
7. applause	_____	g.	a show where people act, sing, or dance
8. orchestra	_____	h.	a place for plays, movies or shows
9. conductor	_____	i.	popular music, movies, and trends
10. exhibition	_____	j.	the people watching or listening to a show

Grammar Focus 1:

Pronouns ending in ***-self*** or ***-selves*** are called reflexive pronouns (재귀대명사) (e.g., *myself, yourself, herself, himself, itself, ourselves, yourselves, themselves*). Reflexive pronouns usually refer back to the subject of a clause or sentence.

e.g., He really loves ***himself***.

You need to serve ***yourself***.

They helped ***themselves*** to the coffee.

Pattern Practice 1:

Fill in the blanks with the correct reflexive pronouns.

1. You should be proud of ______________ for completing a full marathon.
2. She found ______________ lost in the museum.
3. They blamed ______________ for the mistake.
4. I served ______________ at the buffet.
5. Mike really cut ____________ badly when he was slicing the carrots.
6. The theater doesn't have a parking lot attendant, so people must park ____________.
7. My cat accidentally locked ____________ in the room for ten minutes.
8. Minji bought a gift for ______________.
9. My dog always barks at ______________ in a mirror.
10. Can you find ______________ in the group photo?

Grammar Focus 2:

Object pronouns are used as the object of a verb (동사) or preposition (전치사). Specifically, reflexive pronouns are a type of object pronoun used to refer back to the subject of the sentence.

Object Pronouns: ***me, you, him, her, it, us, them*** *Example Sentence:* The teacher called ***you***.
Reflexive Pronouns: ***myself, yourself, himself, herself, itself, ourselves, yourselves, themselves*** *Example Sentence:* I hurt ***myself*** while playing soccer.

Pattern Practice 2:

Fill in the blanks with the correct pronouns.

1. I gave __________ a book to read. **(you/yourself)**
2. They told __________ the story of their travels in Africa. **(me/myself)**
3. We met __________ at the bus stop. **(him/himself)**
4. He encouraged __________ to participate in the activity. **(them/themselves)**
5. People need to serve __________ at a buffet restaurant because there's no one to bring the food to them. **(them/themselves)**
6. I invited __________ to the party. **(her/herself)**
7. She told __________ about the meeting time. **(him/himself)**
8. No one blamed Jack for the mistake, but he blamed __________. **(him/himself)**
9. Please join __________ for lunch next week. **(us/ourselves)**
10. Can I ask __________ a question about the presentation? **(you/yourself)**

Dialogue (Listening and Speaking):

Listen to the dialogue and fill in the missing words. Then practice the dialogue with a partner.

Weekend Plans

Jin: Hey, Mike! The weekend is coming up. Do you have any plans?

Mike: Not yet. I am thinking of doing something fun. What about you?

Jin: I heard there's a concert in the park on (1) ____________________. Do you want to go?

Mike: That sounds great! What kind of music is it?

Jin: It's a (2) _______________ and it's free! We can bring some snacks and enjoy the music.

Mike: Good idea! What else should we do?

Jin: How about a soccer match on Sunday evening ? I saw the ad and thought to (3) ___________________ it would be exciting.

Mike: Oh, I love soccer! But do we still have time to (4) ________________?

Jin: Yes, I checked online this morning. We can get the tickets online and give (5) ________________ enough time to **grab** dinner **beforehand**.

Mike: Awesome! This weekend is going to be **packed**: a concert and soccer. It is going to be amazing!

Jin: Of course. We'll enjoy (6) __________________ this weekend!

Key words: grab 간단하게 먹다 / beforehand 미리 / packed 일정이 꽉 차 있다

Reading: Read the passage and answer the questions.

Mell is an actress. She isn't famous, but she pushes herself harder than other actresses. She gained a lot of weight recently because she needed to **bulk up** for her role in the movie. For breakfast, she eats six eggs and lots of bacon. Then she spends time memorizing difficult lines. Before rehearsal, she stops at a fast-food restaurant and **challenges** herself by eating two hamburgers, finishing every bite.

Today, Mell is filming a challenging restaurant scene where she must make herself stumble onto the floor. In the evening, she feels very proud of herself for having **completed** her role in the movie. **Even though** she's now very overweight, Mell remains dedicated to her job and fully commits herself to her work.

Key words: bulk up 몸집을 키우다 / challenge 도전하다 / completed 완수했다 / even though 비록 ~이지만

Reading Questions: Answer the following questions.

1. Why did Mell gain weight recently?

____

2. What does Mell eat for breakfast?

____

3. What challenge does Mell face before rehearsal?

____

4. What happens in the restaurant scene Mell is filming today?

____

5. How does Mell feel about completing her role in the movie?

____

Conversation Practice:

Work together with your partner and ask each other the following questions.

1. What is your favorite type of entertainment?

   ____

2. Who is your favorite actor or actress?

   ____

3. What was the last movie you saw?

   ____

4. What is your favorite television program?

   ____

5. Who is your favorite musician or singer?

   ____

Exercises

Editing: Correct the following sentences using object pronouns or reflexive pronouns.

1. The young man broke a glass and cut him very badly.

   ____

2. The girl hurt her while playing baseball.

   ____

3. Can you help myself with the assignment?

   ____

4. She trusted himself to deal with the situation.

   ____

5. I saw himself at the library last week.

   ____

Sentence Scramble:

Try to rearrange the words in each scrambled sentence to form a correct sentence.

1. themselves / by / the concert tickets / Sue and Frank / booked

   ____

2. the cake / herself / made / she / by

   ____

3. my friend / talks / he's / to himself / when / nervous

   ____

4. enjoyed / the children / the amusement park / themselves / at

   ____

5. the students / they / should / themselves / when / feel stressed / take care of

   ____

Unit 03

Did you watch the news about the heatwaves?

Warm up:

Try to think about the word 'environment'. In the first bubble, write words related to the environment, such as 'trees', 'pollution', or 'recycling'. In the second bubble, write short actions you can take to protect the environment, such as 'saving water' or 'planting trees'.

Environment

trees *pollution* *recycle*	*saving water* *planting trees*
Words related to the environment	Simple ways to help the environment

Unit 03

Vocabulary: Match the English words with their Korean meanings.

1. pollution	_____	a. 산불
2. ecosystem	_____	b. 생태계
3. recycling	_____	c. 보존
4. reforestation	_____	d. 재활용
5. renewable energy	_____	e. 지속 가능성
6. greenhouse gases	_____	f. 온실가스
7. conservation	_____	g. 재생 가능한 에너지(재생에너지)
8. wildfires	_____	h. 오염
9. sustainability	_____	i. 기후 변화
10. climate change	_____	j. 숲 되살리기

Grammar Focus:

Subject-verb agreement means that the subject and verb in a sentence must match in number. In the present tense, if the subject is singular, the verb must be singular; if the subject is plural, the verb must also be plural.

e.g., ***She is*** happy to learn about pollution. (singular subject-singular verb)

They are happy to learn about pollution. (plural subject-plural verb)

He plants trees every year. (singular subject-singular verb)

They plant trees every year. (plural subject-plural verb)

Singular/Plural	Subject	Be - Verb	Do/Does	Has/Have	Action Verb
Singular	I	am	do	have	e.g., cry, talk
Singular	He/She/It	is	does	has	e.g., cries, talks (Add -s)
Plural	We/They/You	are	do	have	e.g., cry, talk

**You* can be both singular and plural.

Unit 03

Pattern Practice:

Fill in the blanks with the correct subject-verb agreement form based on the present tense.

1. She ________________ learning about climate change. **(enjoy)**
2. My friends ________________ to discuss the ecosystem. **(like)**
3. You ________________ to recycle to reduce pollution. **(need)**
4. Sujin ________________ reforestation every day. **(study)**
5. Many animals ________________ to survive due to wildfires. **(struggle)**
6. The children ________________ about renewable energy at school. **(learn)**
7. I ________________ researching climate change now. **(be)**
8. My brother ________________ about recycling paper. **(care)**
9. It ________________ a lot of wildfires in the summer. **(cause)**
10. They usually________________ about the greenhouse effect. **(talk)**
11. The student ________________ the importance of conservation. **(understand)**
12. We ________________ planning to discuss climate change next month. **(be)**
13. Jack ________________ an assignment related to renewable energy. **(have)**
14. He ________________ focusing on sustainability in his studies. **(be)**
15. Wildfires ________________ quickly in natural areas. **(spread)**

Dialogue (Listening and Speaking):

Listen to the dialogue and fill in the missing words. Then practice the dialogue with a partner.

Alex: Hi, Emma. Did you watch the news about the recent (1) ______________?

Minji: Yeah, it's shocking. People said it's the worst event in years.

Alex: It's all because of global warming. The planet is getting hotter every year, and it's speeding up faster than earlier models predicted.

Minji: I know, it's not just **heatwaves**. (2) ___________ ___________ is leading to more intense storms, higher sea levels, and even **droughts** in some areas.

Alex: Exactly. And the wildfires this year have been terrible, burning for months due to the **extreme** heat and dry conditions.

Minji: Yes, and the **floods** in Asia last month (3) ________________ so many homes. It's heartbreaking.

Alex: I think we need to do our part to reduce **carbon emissions** and encourage governments to act faster.

Minji: You're right. I started recycling, using public transportation, and switching to (4) ___________________ appliances. What about you?

Alex: I'm trying to use less plastic and support (5) ____________________ projects. Every small action counts, but we also need to work together.

Minji: Absolutely. If we don't act now, these extreme weather events will keep getting worse. The future depends on the choices we make today.

Key words: heatwaves 폭염 / droughts 가뭄 / extreme 극단적인 / floods 홍수 / carbon emissions 탄소배출

Reading: Read the passage and answer the questions.

Our earth is facing significant environmental **challenges**, primarily due to pollution. Harmful substances like chemicals and plastics are introduced into the environment at alarming rates. This pollution is affecting the ecosystems.

One major cause of environmental damage is the rise in greenhouse gases like CO2 and methane, which contribute to global warming. In the oceans, too much CO2 makes the water more **acidic**, harming marine life and ecosystems.

To solve these problems, sustainability is important. It means meeting our needs today without harming the future. We can support sustainability by recycling, which turns old materials into new products, reducing waste and saving resources. Using renewable energy like solar, wind, or water power also helps reduce our **reliance** on **fossil fuels**.

Now is the time to take action to protect our planet for future generations.

Key words: challenges 어려움, 도전 / acidic 산성의 / reliance 의존 / fossil fuel 화석연료

Reading Questions: Answer the following questions.

1. What is one major cause of environmental damage?

   ____

2. What happens in the oceans when there is too much CO_2?

   ____

3. What does sustainability mean?

   ____

4. How can we support sustainability?

   ____

5. How can using renewable energy help protect the environment?

   ____

Writing Practice:

Write 5 sentences with the correct subject-verb agreement form.

1. ______________________________
2. ______________________________
3. ______________________________
4. ______________________________
5. ______________________________

Exercises

Editing: Find the errors and correct them in the following sentences, focusing on the present tense.

1. She enjoy joining clean-up activities on weekends.
2. My friend have a warming a hybrid-car.
3. They is excited about the environmental project.
4. He do research on renewable energy.
5. We likes to learn about climate change.

Sentence Scramble:

Try to rearrange the words in each scrambled sentence to form a correct sentence.

1. full / bins / the recycling /are

   ____

2. trees / participated / Jenny / in / planting

   ____

3. in / sings / the bird / the forest

   ____

4. events / join / summer / the students / every / clean-up

   ____

5. paper / enjoys / with / my sister / recycling / her friends

   ____

Unit 04

What's your daily routine?

Warm up: Write three things you do in your daily routine.

Examples: wake up early, eat breakfast, go to school, study in the library, exercise in the afternoon, watch YouTube, go to bed late, etc.

1. ______________________________
2. ______________________________
3. ______________________________

Vocabulary: Match the expression with a similar meaning.

1. bring a lunch box _____ a. carry a lunch box / b. make lunch
2. hang out _____ a. spend time with friends / b. hang up
3. eat out _____ a. cook a home meal / b. have a meal outside
4. sleep in _____ a. get up late / b. sleep over
5. commute _____ a. travel to school / b. work on the computer
6. wash one's face _____ a. face off against / b. clean one's face
7. go to class _____ a. attend class / b. pop up
8. get dressed _____ a. put on clothes / b. buy a dress
9. surf the Internet _____ a. use the Internet / b. surf the channel
10. put on makeup _____ a. apply makeup / b. remove makeup

Grammar Focus:

Let's learn about linking verbs (연결동사) and complements (보어). A complement is a word or group of words that completes the meaning of a sentence by providing additional information about the subject, object, or verb.

Here are some words that are used as linking verbs:

- ***be*** verbs (***e.g.,*** *am, is, are, was, were, being, been*)
- other verbs (***e.g.,*** *appear, become, grow, feel, remain, seem, stay, make, taste, smell, sound, look, etc.*)

This is the basic sentence pattern of linking verbs.

Subject-Linking Verb-Noun (renames the subject)

Subject-Linking Verb-Adjective (describes the subject)

Here are some examples.

Subject	Linking Verb	**Noun** (as a Complement)
John	is	a student
I	am	Susan
You	are	a doctor

Subject	Linking Verb	**Adjective** (as a Complement)
He	looks	ill
It	smells	good
We	grew	tired
I	feel	better today
The music	sounds	great
She	is	tall

Unit 04

Pattern Practice:

Fill in the blanks with the correct linking verb to complete the sentence. There can be more than one appropriate linking verb.

e.g., The children _are/look/feel_ happy to have Christmas presents.

1. The girls ________________ very happy to go skating.
2. The sky ________________ blue.
3. I don't ________________ so good today.
4. She ________________ my classmate.
5. The chicken soup ________________ delicious.
6. They ________________ college students.
7. The movie ________________ interesting.
8. The children ________________ excited about the trip.
9. Your idea ________________ great.
10. Sumi ________________ tired after the workout.

Dialogue (Listening and Speaking):

Listen to the dialogue model and fill in the missing words. Then practice the dialogue with a partner.

Reporter: Hello! Thank you for agreeing to this interview with the Shingu College Newspaper. Let's start by talking about your **daily routine.** What time do you usually get up?

Sumin: I usually get up at 7 o'clock since my first class usually starts at 9a.m. On weekends, I (1) ______________ and have brunch. On weekdays, I usually have (2) ____________________ for breakfast and make lunch to take to school.

Reporter: Do you prepare your own lunch? That's **impressive!**

Sumin: Yes, my lunch is usually **fried rice** with fruit or **leftovers.** I sometimes have food at the school cafeteria or (3) __________________.

Reporter: What do you do after that?

Sumin: After preparing my lunch, I (4) _____________________ , (5) _______________ makeup, and (6) ______________________. Then, I leave for school.

Reporter: How long does it take to get to school?

Sumin: It usually takes about 30 minutes by bus.

Reporter: I see. What do you do when you get to school?

Sumin: I go to class right away, and have lunch with my friends. Then, I attend another lecture or two.

Reporter: What do you usually do in the evening?

Sumin: In the evening, I go to my part-time job. I have to support myself because I live on my own.

Reporter: Wow, you have such a busy day. When do you hang out with your friends?

Sumin: On Friday afternoons, I (7) ______________________ my friends to visit popular restaurants or sometimes go for **draft beer** and fried chicken.

Reporter:	What else do you do in your free time?
Sumin:	I like to (8) ______________________ and spend time watching *YouTube*.
Reporter:	How many hours of sleep do you usually get?
Sumin:	It depends, but I usually sleep 7 to 8 hours.
Reporter:	Sumin, thank you for sharing your daily routine today! This will be really helpful for writing an article about "A day in the life of a college student."
Sumin:	You're very welcome. I'm looking forward to reading it.

Key words: daily routine 하루 일과 / impressive 인상깊은 / fried rice 볶음밥 / leftovers 남은 음식 / draft beer 생맥주

Reading: Read the passage and answer the questions.

Australian university students start their days early when they have morning lectures. They commute to campus using public transport, bikes, or by walking. After attending lectures or **tutorials**, they usually take a lunch break at campus cafes. Some students bring lunchboxes with a variety of foods, such as sandwiches, fried rice, **stir-fried noodles**, or salads. They spend their afternoons attending additional classes, participating in study groups, or working on **assignments**. Students often **balance** part-time jobs, sports, and socializing at pubs or beaches during their spare time. Managing academics, work, and free time can be challenging, but it's an **essential** aspect of their dynamic university life.

Key words: tutorials 소규모 강의 / stir-fried noodles 볶음면 / assignments 과제 / balance 균형을 맞추다 / essential 필수적인

Reading Questions: Answer the following questions.

1. How do students commute to campus?

____

2. Where do students usually take their lunch break?

____

3. What kind of food do some students bring for lunch?

____

4. What do students do in the afternoons?

____

5. How do students spend their spare time?

____

Unit 04

Conversation Practice: Work together with a partner and ask each other these questions.

1. What time do you usually get up in the morning?

   ____

2. What do you usually have for breakfast?

   ____

3. How do you get to school?

   ____

4. How do you spend your afternoons?

   ____

5. What do you do for fun?

   ____

Exercises

Editing: Correct the following sentences using what you have learned in this unit.

1. He are happy after the meeting.

   ____

2. The weather smells nice today.

   ____

3. The flowers feels wonderful in the garden.

   ____

4. The apple pie feels delicious.

   ____

5. My sister were excited about her holidays.

   ____

Sentence Scramble:

Try to rearrange the words in each scrambled sentence to form a correct sentence.

1. for a picnic / the weather / perfect / seems

2. famous / she / writer / became / a

3. appears / cloudy / the sky / today

4. happy / the new job / my sister / with / looks

5. after / feel / the long day / I / tired

Unit 05

Have you heard of K-culture?

Warm up:

Think about what you know about K-culture. In pairs or small groups, ask and answer these questions:

출처: BTS 공식홈페이지

- What comes to your mind when you hear K-culture?
- Have you explained any part of K-culture, such as K-pop, K-dramas or food, to non-Koreans?
- If you were to talk about K-culture to non-Koreans, what would you like to talk about the most?
- Why do you think K-culture is popular worldwide?

Try to share an interesting answer with the class!

Vocabulary:

Match the English words with their Korean meanings.

1. cuisine	_____	a. 영향(을 주다)
2. popularity	_____	b. 기억에 남는, 인상적인
3. Korean wave	_____	c. 음식, 요리
4. skincare	_____	d. 인기
5. influence	_____	e. 관심
6. beauty products	_____	f. 한류
7. entertainment	_____	g. 피부 관리
8. attention	_____	h. 세계적 확산
9. memorable	_____	i. 화장품
10. global spread	_____	j. 오락

Grammar Focus:

Let's learn about ***quantifiers*** (수량사).

1) ***many*** vs. ***much***
2) ***few / a few*** vs. ***little / a little***
3) ***lots of / a lot of***

	Used with Countable Nouns		Used with Uncountable Nouns
many	I have **many** friends.	*much*	I have **much** gratitude for your kindness.
	There are **many** books on the shelf.		There is **much** information about the topic.
a lot of / lots of is used with both countable and uncountable nouns. There are **a lot of** students in the classroom. Jenny has **lots of** energy even after a long day.			
few / a few	There are **few** chairs in the meeting room.	*little / a little*	I have **little** information on this issue.
	She has **a few** friends.		He spent **a little** money on groceries this week.

Many, few, and ***a few*** are followed by plural nouns, while ***much, little,*** and ***a little*** are followed by singular (uncountable) nouns. ***A lot of*** and ***lots of*** can be followed by both singular (uncountable) and plural nouns.

Pattern Practice:

Fill in the blanks with the correct word : ***many, much, a few, few, a little or little.***

- Complete the following sentences with ***many*** or ***much***.

1. There are ______________ people at the Christmas concert.
2. We drank too ______________ coffee at the meeting.
3. I saw ______________ birds flying over the lake.
4. Don't feel ________________ pressure to succeed.
5. There isn't ______________ sugar left in the jar.

- Complete the following sentences with ***a few / few*** or ***a little / little***.

1. I need ________________ minutes to think about it.
2. Lynn liked sweet coffee, so she added ________________ sugar to her tea.
3. Minsu made ________________ mistakes during the presentation, but it was good.
4. Sarah feels sad because she has ________________ friends who understand her well.
5. He had ________________ chance of winning the tennis match, but he did his best.

Dialogue (Listening and Speaking):

Listen to the dialogue model and fill in the missing words. Then practice the dialogue with a partner.

Jun: Have you heard of K-culture? It is becoming more popular and (1) ________________ in many areas.

Kelly: Yes, I know. (2) ________________ people are talking about Korean music, dramas, food, and even beauty.

Jun: I agree! I think K-pop is the biggest part of it. Groups like *BTS* and *BLACKPINK* have (3) ________________ fans all over the world. Their music videos are so cool and memorable.

Kelly: Yeah, their music videos are **awesome**. I started watching K-dramas. *Goblin* and *Descendants of the Sun* are really fun.

Jun: Wow, that's great! Korean dramas are receiving (4) ________________ attention.

Kelly: Right. I think K-dramas show Korean life and **blend** romance, humor, and **sorrow**. Recently, I tried to make *kimchi* at home and I love *tteokbokki*(떡볶이) and *bibimbap*(비빔밥).

Jun: Wow, it's also fun to try all the side dishes, called *banchan*(반찬) in Korean. They come with the meal. And I heard that Korean skincare and K-beauty products are becoming very popular too.

Kelly: Yes, K-beauty products are good and (5) ________________. I often talk about Korean **cosmetics** with my friends back home.

Jun: Really? K-culture, including cosmetics, has become more than just (6) ________________. While talking about K-culture, I've become hungry. Why don't we have *kimbap*(김밥) and *ramen*(라면) for lunch?

Kelly: That's a brilliant idea!

Key words: awesome 멋진 / blend 섞다 / sorrow 슬픔 / cosmetics 화장품

Reading: Read the passage and answer the questions.

K-culture refers to cultural elements from South Korea. In recent years, it has gained global popularity. K-dramas like *Squid Game*(오징어게임) and *My Love from the Star*(별에서 온 그대) have **attracted** worldwide attention. Many people around the world enjoy watching the program *Infinite Challenge*(무한도전), a popular South Korean television variety show. They turn on the **subtitles** while watching Korean TV programs to understand the content.

They also study the Korean language through these programs. Korean beauty products, known for their effectiveness, are becoming increasingly popular. In addition, traditional dishes like *bulgogi*(불고기), *kimchi*(김치), and *bibimbap*(비빔밥) are also gaining popularity. People around the world are **embracing** the Korean language and culture. This global **excitement**, called the 'Korean Wave', keeps growing, blending modern and traditional aspects to create a unique cultural **identity**.

Key words: attracted (관심을) 끄는 / subtitles 자막 / embracing 포용하는 / excitement 열정 / identity 정체성

Reading Questions: Answer the following questions.

1. What is K-culture?

   ____

2. Which K-dramas are mentioned in the passage?

   ____

3. What is *Infinite Challenge*?

   ____

4. How do foreign people understand Korean TV programs?

   ____

5. What aspects of Korean culture are gaining global popularity?

   ____

Conversation Practice:

Work together with a partner and ask each other these questions.

1. Which K-pop groups do you like?

 ____

2. What is your favorite K-drama or TV show?

 ____

3. What is your favorite Korean food?

 ____

4. What Korean beauty products do you usually use?

 ____

5. Why do you think K-culture is so popular worldwide?

 ____

Exercises

Editing:

Correct the following sentences using ***many, much, (a) few*** or ***(a) little***.

1. A little people like to travel during the holidays.

   ____

2. She drank too many water after hiking.

   ____

3. The professor encouraged the students to ask much questions, but they asked little questions during the lecture.

   ____

4. How many flour do you need?

   ____

5. I tried to find information about the topic, but I couldn't find many information about that topic online.

   ____

Sentence Scramble:

Try to rearrange the words in each scrambled sentence to form a correct sentence.

1. pizza / at the party / ate / lots of / we

   ____

2. are / people / there / in the meeting / many / room / how

   ____

3. her / she / have / much / to finish / doesn't / homework / time

   ____

4. in / there / water / is / the bottle / little

   ____

5. finish / his work / feels / a lot of / he / pressure / to

   ____

Unit 06

Review

Unit 01 : How's college life going?

Vocabulary: Write the English word for each Korean meaning.

1. 강의계획서 ________________
2. 학기 ________________
3. 체육대회 ________________
4. 취업박람회 ________________
5. 중간고사 ________________
6. 기말고사 ________________
7. 과외 활동 ________________
8. 학생회관 ________________
9. 동아리 박람회 ________________
10. 학교 식당의 음식 (학식) ________________

Grammar: Make a question that begins with ***who, what, when, where, why,*** or ***how*** to match the given answer. Then, practice asking and answering the questions with your partner.

1. ____?
   She is studying.
2. ____? (did)
   I bought this at a grocery store.
3. ____? (does)
   My class begins at 12:35.
4. ____? (did)
   I came here by bus.
5. ____? (did)
   Because I wanted to see my friends.

Conversation Practice: Ask the following questions to your partner and write down their answers. Then, switch roles.

1. Who is your favorite athlete?
   ____
2. Why do you like them?
   ____
3. What is your favorite season?
   ____
4. Why did you choose your current major?
   ____
5. How do you usually spend your weekends?
   ____

Unit 02: Are you going to enjoy yourself this weekend?

Vocabulary: Write the English word for each Korean meaning.

1. 연극 ____________________
2. 극장 ____________________
3. 박수 ____________________
4. 공연 ____________________
5. 대중 문화 ____________________
6. 오케스트라 ____________________
7. 전시회 ____________________
8. 관객, 청중 ____________________
9. 지휘자 ____________________
10. 유명인 ____________________

Grammar: Fill in the blanks with the correct object pronouns (*me, you, her, him...*) or reflexive pronouns (*myself, yourself, herself, himself...*).

1. No one praised Sumi for finishing her project, but Sumi is proud of ______________. **(her/herself)**
2. We have to serve ______________ at the buffet. **(us/ourselves)**
3. He always plays computer games by ______________. **(him/himself)**
4. Because there was no host, the presenters introduced ______________ to the group. **(them/themselves)**
5. Jenny went on a trip alone, and she found ______________ lost in the new city. **(her/herself)**
6. I will meet ______________ at the top of the mountain. **(you/yourself)**
7. He showed ______________ the way to the museum. **(her/herself)**
8. The secretary told ______________ about the meeting time. **(him/himself)**
9. My friend likes to tell ______________ the story of his travels. **(me/myself)**
10. May I ask ______________ a question? **(you/yourself)**

Writing: Write 5 sentences using the reflexive pronouns (*myself, yourself, herself, himself,* and *themselves*).

1. ______________________________

2. ______________________________

3. ______________________________

4. ______________________________

5. ______________________________

Unit 03: Did you watch the news about the heatwaves?

Vocabulary: Write the English word for each Korean meaning.

1. 재활용 ______________________
2. 온실가스 ______________________
3. 산불 ______________________
4. 보존, 보호 ______________________
5. 생태계 ______________________
6. 숲 복원 ______________________
7. 지속 가능성 ______________________
8. 기후 변화 ______________________
9. 오염 ______________________
10. 재생 가능 에너지 ______________________

Grammar: Fill in the blanks with the correct subject-verb agreement form based on the present tense.

1. Pollution ________________ animals and plants. **(harm)**
2. Trees ________________ us oxygen to breathe. **(give)**
3. Wildfires ________________quickly in dry forests. **(spread)**
4. Climate change ________________weather more extreme. **(make)**
5. Factories ________________ a lot of greenhouse gases. **(produce)**
6. The community ________________ the park every weekend. **(clean)**
7. Water pollution ________________ fish and other sea life. **(affect)**
8. Everyone ________________to help the environment. **(need)**
9. Plastic bags ________________problems for wildlife. **(cause)**
10. Recycling ________________resources and energy. **(save)**

Writing: Write 5 sentences using the correct subject-verb agreement form in the present tense, as follows.

e.g., She _enjoys_ reading books in her free time.
The flowers _bloom_ beautifully in spring.

1. ____
2. ____
3. ____
4. ____
5. ____

Unit 04 : What's your daily routine?

Vocabulary: Write the English word for each Korean meaning.

1. 옷을 입다 ______________________
2. 외식하다 ______________________
3. 인터넷을 검색하다 ______________________
4. 도시락을 가져오다 ______________________
5. 통학(통근)하다 ______________________
6. 늦잠을 자다 ______________________
7. 수업에 가다 ______________________
8. (친구들과) 어울리다, 놀다 ______________________
9. 화장을 하다 ______________________
10. 세수하다 ______________________

Grammar: Fill in the blanks with the correct linking verb to complete the sentence.

1. We ________________ tired after the long trip.
2. This soup ________________ sour.
3. The weather ________________ perfect for a picnic yesterday.
4. My dog ________________very friendly even to strangers.
5. They ________________ late for the meeting last week.
6. Kate ________________happy after the good news.
7. The flowers ________________good in the garden.
8. The child ________________sleepy after playing soccer.
9. His explanation ________________clear and concise.
10. She ________________ excited about her trip to Africa.

Conversation Practice: Work with a partner and ask each other these questions about your daily routines.

1. What do you usually have for lunch?

   ____

2. How do you get home after school?

   ____

3. Do you prefer to study alone or in a group? Why?

   ____

4. What sports do you play or how do you exercise regularly?

   ____

5. How do you relax after a busy day?

   ____

Unit 05: Have you heard of K-culture?

Vocabulary: Write the English word for each Korean meaning.

1. 관심 ______________________
2. 기억에 남는, 인상적인 ______________________
3. 인기 ______________________
4. 세계적 확산 ______________________
5. 음식, 요리 ______________________
6. 영향(을 주다) ______________________
7. 피부 관리 ______________________
8. 화장품 ______________________
9. 한류 ______________________
10. (영화·음악 등의) 오락(물) ______________________

Grammar: Complete the following sentences with ***many*** or ***much***.

1. Anne bought ____________ apples at the supermarket.
2. We don't have ____________ time to finish this task.
3. Minsu has ____________ friends in his class.
4. I ate too ____________ cake at the party.
5. He has ____________ homework to do this weekend.

Complete the following sentences with ***a few*** or ***a little***.

6. We have ________________ free time this afternoon.

7. Jack has ________________ money left in his wallet.

8. There are ________________ eggs left in the refrigerator.

9. Some students need ________________ help with their assignment.

10. There are ________________ chairs in the meeting room.

Conversation Practice: Work with a partner and ask each other these questions about K-culture.

1. Which K-pop songs do you listen to the most?

____

2. What Korean street food do you like the most?

____

3. What Korean fashion styles do you like?

____

4. Have you ever attended a K-pop concert or fan meeting?

____

5. Do you enjoy watching Korean variety shows? If so, which one?

____

Unit 07

What do you want to do?

Warm up: Write three plans you have for yourself within the next 5 years.

Examples: find a job, go to graduate school or study more, get an A grade at school, travel abroad, obtain a certification, get a driver's license.

1. ______________________________

2. ______________________________

3. ______________________________

Vocabulary: Match the verbs to the meanings.

1. want _____
2. expect _____
3. need _____
4. forget _____
5. plan _____
6. decide _____
7. hope _____
8. like _____
9. love _____
10. hate _____

a. 계획하다
b. 필요하다
c. 희망하다
d. 잊다
e. 결정하다
f. 원하다
g. 예상하다
h. 사랑하다
i. 싫어하다
j. 좋아하다

Grammar Focus: Infinitives (부정사)

An ***infinitive (to-infinitive = to Verb)*** is a grammar word. It is formed by *to + the base form of a verb* (동사원형).

For example: to eat, to run, to play, to learn

Infinitive = *to + simple form of a verb*

Subject	Verb	Infinitive	
He	wants	to go	to the park.
She	needs	to quit	smoking.
You	would like	to see	the show.
They	plan	to travel	in the summer.
We	decided	to have	dinner.
I	hope	to win	the soccer game.

Pattern Practice 1: Underline the verbs and circle the infinitives. 

Example: The students <u>*hope*</u> (to find) a job soon.

1. I want to eat pizza for dinner tonight.
2. She loves to go to the beach on the weekends.
3. We need to buy groceries for the week.
4. He will try to learn Spanish before his trip to Mexico.
5. They plan to visit their grandparents next month.
6. She decided to study medicine in college.
7. I hope to travel to Japan someday.
8. He hates to sleep after eating a big meal.
9. She would like to learn how to play the guitar.
10. We like to clean the house before guests arrive.

Pattern Practice 2: Fill in the blanks using the correct verb. Remember to add an 's' to the verbs when using *he, she,* and *it*.

Example: I <u>*love*</u> to eat popcorn at the movie theater. (매우 좋아하다)

1. I ________________ to become fluent in French. (원하다)
2. They ________________ to find the lost puppy. (희망하다)
3. We ________________ to watch a movie tonight after dinner. (계획하다)
4. Lisa ________________ to bake cookies for a party. (좋아하다)

Pattern Practice 3: Translate the following sentences to English. 

Example: 저는 유럽으로 여행하고 싶습니다.

I would like to travel to Europe.

1. 저는 새 차를 사고 싶어요. **(want)**

   ____

2. 그는 집에 가야 돼요. **(need)**

   ____

3. 저는 저녁식사로 후라이드 치킨을 먹고 싶습니다. **(would like)**

   ____

4. BTS는 많은 팬들을 만나길 희망해요. **(hope)**

   ____

5. 내 친구들과 나는 해변으로 가기로 결정했어요. **(decided)**

   ____

Dialogue (Listening and Speaking):

Listen to the dialogue and fill in the missing words. Then practice the dialogue with your partner twice.

Jin: Have you thought about what you want to do after we **graduate**?

Sue: Yeah, I thought a lot about it. I (1) ____________________ a job in Seoul.

Jin: Cool! What kind of job would you like to have?

Sue: I'd really love to work in graphic design or in something related to technology. What about you? Have you made any **decisions** about what you would like to do?

Jin: Yeah, I have (2) ____________________ my own business. I hope to open a cafe.

Sue: That's exciting! I (3) ____________________ your first **customer** when you open!

Jin: Thank you! I appreciate your **support**. Do you think finding a job will be hard?

Sue: It might be, but I'm quite diligent. I plan to start my job search this weekend. And what about you? Do you think you'll like running your own cafe?

Jin: I think so. I'm a coffee **connoisseur**. I hope to make it a pleasant place for people to relax.

Sue: That sounds great! I (4) ____________________ and try your menu. Don't (5) ____________________ a wide selection of teas. I hate to go to cafes where they don't serve a wide selection of items on their menu.

Jin: Thanks for the advice, Sue. Yes, I agree with you. I do love to drink both tea and coffee. I expect to see you at my cafe in the future!

Key words: graduate 졸업하다 / decision 결정 / customer 손님 / support 지원 / connoisseur 전문가

Reading: Read the following story. Write full-sentence answers to the questions.

Making a Difference

Volunteering is a meaningful way to make a difference in our **communities** and help people in need.

People like to volunteer for a variety of reasons. Some people decide to help clean up parks and streets. They want to make their neighborhoods cleaner and more attractive.

Other people like to spend their time helping elderly people. **Elders** need to talk to people because they can be lonely. We need to remember that our elders have **wisdom** to share. They need to get our respect and care.

Often, young people plan to volunteer at **animal shelters**. They plan to play with the animals and feed them. They want to keep the animals safe and happy.

We can make the world a better place for everyone when we volunteer. We can volunteer to help people, animals, or our communities. Most people don't want to live in a world where no one helps to make things better and more **equitable**.

Key words: volunteering 자원 봉사 / communities 지역 사회 / elders 노인들 / wisdom 지혜 / animal shelters 동물 보호소 / equitable 공정한

Reading Questions:

1. Why do some people want to help clean up parks and streets?

 ____

2. What do young people plan to do at animal shelters?

 ____

3. Why do elders need to talk to people?

 ____

4. What do we need to remember about our elders?

 ____

Conversation Practice: Work together with a partner. Ask and answer the following questions. Use Infinitives ***(to-infinitive = to Verb)*** in your answers (to + verb).

e.g., I want _*to watch*_ TV.

1. What do you want to do this weekend?

 ____

2. What would you like to eat for dinner?

 ____

3. What do you need to study this week?

 ____

4. Where do you plan to travel next vacation?

 ____

5. What do you hope to be in the future?

 ____

Editing: Find and correct the errors in the following sentences.

1. She want to go to the store after school.

   ____

2. He needs study more for the exam tomorrow.

   ____

3. I try to learns Japanese on the weekends.

   ____

4. We hope to goes camping this summer.

   ____

5. They would like traveling around the world someday.

   ____

Writing Time:

Make your own sentences using the infinitive.

1. I want to______________________________

2. This weekend, I need to ______________________________

3. ______________________________

4. ______________________________

5. ______________________________

Unit 08

Do you enjoy being active?

Warm up: What activities and exercises do you enjoy?

Check the ones you enjoy doing and make sentences with your partner.

Example: I enjoy _walking._

Vocabulary: Common Gerund Verbs

Match the verbs to their meanings.

1. enjoy	_____	a. 시작하다
2. avoid	_____	b. 그만두다
3. (don't) mind	_____	c. 유지하다
4. start	_____	d. 피하다
5. finish	_____	e. 즐기다
6. keep	_____	f. 신경 쓰다
7. quit	_____	g. 끝내다
8. like	_____	h. 사랑하다
9. love	_____	i. 싫어하다
10. hate	_____	j. 좋아하다

Grammar Focus 1: Gerunds 동명사 (*Verb + ing*)

Gerund is a grammar word. A gerund is a *verb* form that ends in ***-ing*** and is used as a *noun*. It can act as the subject, object, or complement in a sentence.

Examples:

1. **Subject:** *Swimming* is my favorite hobby.
   (*Swimming* is the activity being talked about.)
2. **Object:** I enjoy *reading*.
   (*Reading* is what I enjoy.)
3. **Complement:** My favorite activity is *dancing*.
   (*Dancing* describes the favorite activity.)

A *gerund* looks like the *present participle* (현재분사, *Verb + -ing)* but it works as a noun, not a verb.

You can often put a *gerund* where you would use a *noun* in a sentence.

Gerund = (simple form of a verb + ***-ing***)

Subject	Verb	Gerund	
He	enjoys	go**ing**	to baseball games.
She	starts	studying	for the test.
You	quit	drinking	soda.
They	finished	doing	their homework.
We	avoid	going	to noisy places.
I	keep	trying	to call him.

Pattern Practice 1: Fill in the blanks using a verb from vocabulary section 1.

Example: They _like_ going for walks in the park. (좋아하다)

1. I ______________________ reading books in my free time. (즐기다)
2. He __________________________ practicing the piano. (끝내다)
3. They __________________________ eating with dirty hands. (싫어하다)
4. She __________________________ working at her job last week. (그만두다)
5. I _______________________ waking up early on the weekends. (피하다)

Grammar Focus 2: *to -Infinitive* and *Gerunds* (*to* 부정사, 동명사)

to-Infinitives (Unit 7):

Remember what you have learned in unit 7. ***to-infinitives*** are formed by ***to*** + the base form of a verb)

For example: to eat, to run, to play, to learn

Gerunds (Unit 8):

A ***gerund*** is a verb form that ends in "***-ing***" and functions as a ***noun*** in a sentence. Unlike infinitives, gerunds do not require the word "***to***" before them. For example, in the sentence "I like reading", the gerund form of the verb "***read***" is "***reading***".

Infinitives (to + verb)	Both (infinitive or gerund)	Gerunds (verb + *ing*)
want	like, love, hate	enjoy
would like		avoid
need		(don't) mind
forget		start
plan		finish
decide		dislike
hope		quit

Pattern Practice 2: Use the correct infinitive or gerund. 

Example: My friends like _to play/playing_ (play) soccer in the evenings.

1. She needs ______________________ (study) for the test tonight.
2. When I finish ______________________ (write) this letter, I'll help you.
3. I want ______________________ (buy) a new laptop soon.
4. He quit ______________________ (smoke) and feels much better now.
5. We forgot ______________________ (bring) our books to school.
6. They decided ______________________ (travel) to Europe this summer.
7. She avoids ______________________ (walk) in the rain.
8. You need ______________________ (practice) more grammar.
9. I love ______________________ (go) to the mountains.
10. I don't mind ______________________ (watch) scary movies.

Dialogue (Listening and Speaking):

Listen to the dialogue and fill in the missing words. Then practice the dialogue with your partner twice.

Paul: Do you enjoy playing sports, Raymond?

Raymond: Yeah, I really (1) ______________________ soccer. It's so much fun!

Paul: That's great! I want to start playing a new sport. Do you mind giving me some **advice**?

Raymond: Of course, I don't mind helping. What sport are you thinking about starting?

Paul: Well, I'd like to (2) ______________________ . I want to (3) ______________________ tired all the time.

Raymond: That is a great choice! Running is an excellent way to keep fit.

Paul: I decided to (4) ______________________ **excuses** and try it.

Raymond: That's the right **attitude**! Starting is the hardest part, but once you get going, you'll enjoy it. Just (5) ______________________ yourself, and you'll finish feeling like a winner.

Paul: Thanks for the **support**. I'll let you know after I finish my first run.

Raymond: Awesome! I want to hear about it. If you need any advice or support, I'm here to help.

Paul: Thanks, I **appreciate** it.

Key words: advice 조언 / excuses 변명 / attitude 태도 / support 지원 / appreciate 감사하다

Reading: Read the following story. Write full-sentence answers to the questions.

Cathy's Exercise Plan

Cathy wants to be healthy. She doesn't want to feel tired or **lethargic**. As a result, Cathy has a regular exercise plan. In the mornings, she starts stretching to warm up her muscles. After that, she likes to go for a run in the park. Running helps her feel **energetic** and happy.

When she finishes her run, she does some strength exercises. She needs to build strong muscles, so she decides to **lift weights**. She hopes to do many squats and **push-ups** to make her body strong and **fit**.

In the afternoons, Cathy enjoys doing yoga. Yoga helps her relax and stay **flexible**. She follows videos online and tries different poses. She wants to improve her balance through yoga.

In the evenings, Cathy likes going for a walk with her dog. Walking is a simple exercise, but it's good for one's health. Cathy likes spending time outdoors and breathing in the fresh air.

Overall, Cathy tries to exercise every day to stay healthy and happy.

Key words: lethargic 무기력한 / energetic 활발한 / lift weights 아령을 들다 / push-ups 팔굽혀펴기 / fit 몸매가 좋은 / flexible 유연한

Reading Questions:

1. Why does Cathy have a regular exercise plan?

   ____

2. What does she like doing in the mornings?

   ____

3. What does she enjoy doing in the afternoons?

   ____

4. How does yoga help her?

   ____

5. What does she do in the evenings?

   ____

Conversation Practice: Work together with a partner. Ask and answer the following questions. Use ***to-infinitive*** or ***gerund*** in your answers.

1. What activities do you enjoy doing in your free time?

   ____

2. When do you start studying in the day?

   ____

3. When do you finish studying?

   ____

4. What do you do to stay healthy? Do you enjoy playing sports or doing exercise?

   ____

5. How do you avoid feeling stressed?

   ____

*Tip: Remember the rule for talking about sports using the verbs ***play, go*** and ***do***.
We use:
play for ball sports and chess (e.g., *I enjoy playing tennis*)
go if the sport ends in ***-ing*** (e.g., *I like to go swimming*)
do if the sport is an exercise, a solo activity, or a martial art (무술)
(e.g., *I like doing Taekwondo* 태권도)

Editing: Find and correct the errors in the following sentences.

1. He wants to learning how to play soccer.

   ____

2. Sarah loves to dance and singing in the band.

   ____

3. We need buying some groceries for the week.

   ____

4. He hate to wake up early in the morning.

   ____

5. They avoid to do their projects.

   ____

Writing Time:

• Make sentences using the ***gerund***.

1. I enjoy ______________________________

2. I don't mind ______________________________

3. ______________________________

4. ______________________________

5. ______________________________

• Make sentences using ***to-infinitive*** or ***gerund***.

6. ______________________________

7. ______________________________

8. ______________________________

9. ______________________________

10. ______________________________

Unit 09

Have you planned your trip yet?

Warm up: Which type of trip looks more exciting: Picture one or Picture two? Explain your reasons to your partner.

1.

2.

Vocabulary: Travel

Match the words to the meanings. 

1. destination _____
2. itinerary _____
3. reservation _____
4. adventure _____
5. resort _____
6. breathtaking _____
7. crowded _____
8. exhausted _____

a. a planned route or schedule for a trip
b. full of people, often uncomfortably so
c. the place someone is going
d. making you feel calm and free from stress
e. an exciting or unusual experience
f. causing great enthusiasm
g. booking something in advance, e.g., a ticket
h. extremely beautiful or surprising

9. relaxing _____ i. a place where people go to relax

10. exciting _____ j. very tired

Grammar Focus 1: Adjectives (형용사)

A ***noun*** (명사) is a person, place or a thing. e.g., man, woman, pen, resort, beach.

An ***adjective*** (형용사) describes the noun and gives more information about it.

For example: Beautiful beaches (describes the beaches)

Crowded streets (describes the streets)

We can use adjectives in the following ways.

Adjective + noun

An **exciting** adventure

The **busy** tourist

The **quiet** beach

Be verb + adjective.

The views were **pretty**.

The buildings are **beautiful**.

It is **breathtaking**!

Have/has + adjective + noun.

The mountain has **stunning** views.

The city has a **big** population.

I have a **full** itinerary.

Pattern Practice 1: Adjectives

Fill in the blanks with the correct adjectives from the list below. 

breathtaking crowded happy relaxing full
dirty exciting large small unhappy

1. We visited a ________________ mountain village with stunning views.
2. The city square was ____________________ with too many people during the festival.
3. I had a ____________________ day by the pool.
4. The tour guide took us to an _____________________ waterfall.
5. The ________________ streets need to be cleaned.
6. The man has a ___________ itinerary. He will be busy.
7. I am __________. It's my birthday and my vacation will start tomorrow.
8. Korea has a ____________ population compared to China
9. She is _____________. She is sick and she can't take a trip during this vacation.
10. China has a ____________ population compared to Korea.

Grammar Focus 2: *Adjectives* ending in *-ed* and *-ing*

Adjectives ending in ***-ed*** describe emotions; they explain how people feel.

It isn't common to use the ***-ed*** endings to talk about non-living things, so we would use the ***-ed*** ending with the pronouns ***I, you, he, she, they, we***.

Adjectives ending in ***-ing*** describe the thing that causes the feeling. We would commonly use the ***-ing*** ending with the pronoun ***it***.

Examples:

I am **excited** about the journey.

The trip is **exciting**.

He was very **tired** during his holiday at the resort. It was **tiring**.

Pattern Practice 2: Adjectives ending in *-ed* and *-ing*.

Choose the correct word to complete the sentence:

1. The journey was so long that I felt ________________ *(exhausted/exhausting)*

2. The gallery was ________________ *(bored/boring)*, so we left.

3. The travel guide gave us ________________ *(interested/interesting)* advice for our trip.

4. After a joyful day of sightseeing, we felt ________________ *(relaxed/relaxing)*.

5. The city has many ________________ *(excited/exciting)* places to visit.

6. The job in Mexico should be ________________ *(satisfied /satisfying)*.

7. I was *(disappointed/disappointing)* ________________ not to take a holiday this year.

8. It was *(fascinated/fascinating)* ________________ to go on the hiking trail.

9. Are you *(confused/confusing)* ________________ when reading this book?

10. They were *(amazing/amazed)* ________________ to learn the size of the hiking trail.

Dialogue (Listening and Speaking):

Listen to the dialogue and fill in the missing words. Then practice the dialogue with your partner twice.

Sara: Hey, John! Have you planned your vacation yet?

John: Not yet, but I'm thinking about visiting a mountain **resort**.

Sara: That sounds exciting! I am excited for you! Will you go (1)______________ or just relax instead?

John: Both! I've heard the trails are breathtaking.

Sara: Be careful. Some **trails** are (2)______________ if you're not well (3)______________.

John: Good point. I'll pack proper **gear**. What about you?

Sara: I'm going **sightseeing** in Paris. The Eiffel Tower is on my (4)______________.

John: That's amazing! The Eiffel Tower is very **historic**. It has **splendid** views of the beautiful, romantic city. I've heard it can be crowded, though.

Sara: True, but I think it'll still be worth it. It will be a (5)______________ trip.

John: Definitely. Traveling can be so **rewarding**.

Sara: I agree. Enjoy your trip!

Key words: resort 휴양지 / trail 등산로 / gear 의복 / sightseeing 관광 / historic 역사적인 / splendid 멋진 / rewarding 가치가 있는

Conversation Practice: Ask and answer the following questions with your partner.

1. When was your last vacation? Where did you go and what did you do?

   ____

2. Think of three adjectives to describe your trip (e.g., exciting, boring, etc.).

   ____

3. What types of activities do you like to do when you take a trip?

   ____

4. Do you plan to take a trip during the next school vacation?

   ____

5. Where is the best place for sightseeing in Korea?

   ____

Reading: Read the following story. Write full sentence answers to the questions.

What a trip!

Last summer vacation, Lisa planned a trip to Japan. She was extremely excited and happy because she had always wanted to visit Tokyo. It was on her **bucket list**. The city was extremely crowded with **throngs** of people everywhere, but Lisa found it **exhilarating**. She enjoyed visiting famous landmarks like the breathtaking Mount Fuji and the Golden **Pavilion**, a Buddhist temple built in the 14th century. Lisa's itinerary also included a relaxing day at an *onsen*, a traditional Japanese hot spring. She loved spending time at the onsen. It was very refreshing. By the end of the trip, Lisa was exhausted but happy. It was one of the most **memorable** vacations she had ever taken. She can't wait to go back someday!

Key words: bucket list 꼭 해보고 싶은 목록 / throng 군중 / exhilarating 아주 신나는 / pavilion 구조물 / memorable 기억에 남는

Reading Questions:

1. Why was Lisa excited about her trip to Japan?

2. What did she think about Tokyo?

3. Name two places Lisa visited.

4. What is an *onsen*?

5. How did Lisa feel at the end of her trip?

Editing: Find and correct the errors in the following sentences. 

1. The journey was tired.

2. The resort is very relaxing.

3. I am interesting in visiting Italy.

4. The beach was so bored that we left early.

5. The sightseeing tour was exhaust.

Unit 10

This is the teacher *who* helps me.

Warm up: Look at the pictures. Describe each picture using the information below.

출처: BTS 공식홈페이지

1\. 

It's a thing *which*...

____

2\. 

It's a person *who*...

____

Vocabulary: Match the words to the meanings. 

1. heritage _____
2. recipe _____
3. spices _____
4. landmark _____
5. architect _____

a. an area of land

b. something that is passed down from old to young people

c. a building or object that is famous

d. something that has been built

e. something used to flavor food, like red-pepper paste (고추장)

6. cuisine ______
7. skyscraper ______
8. region ______
9. structure ______
10. Ingredient ______

f. instructions for preparing a dish
g. a person who designs buildings
h. a very tall building
i. foods that are combined to make a dish
j. a style of cooking that represents a region

Grammar Focus 1: What are Relative Pronouns (관계대명사)?

Relative Pronouns are words used to connect a description to a ***Noun***. They give more information about people, things, or places.

Common Relative Pronouns

Who : used for people

Which : used for things or animals

That : used for people, things, or animals

Whose : shows possession

Antecedent (선행사)	Subjective Case (주격)	Possessive Case (소유격)	Objective Case (목적격)
People	who/that	whose	who(m), that, ∅
Things/Animals	which/that	whose/of which	which, that, ∅

Look at the following sentences using ***relative pronouns***. The relative pronouns put two ideas together.

Who : **Used for people.**

This is the teacher *who* helps me.

(= This is the teacher. + The teacher helps me.)

Which : **Used for things or animals.** ***Which*** introduces extra, but *not* essential, information and is usually set off by commas.

The bag, *which* is on the chair, is John's.

(= The bag is John's. + The bag is on the chair.)

That : **Used for people, things, or animals.** ***That*** introduces essential information or specifies which one of several things is being talked about. It is usually *not* set off by commas.

This is the dog *that* I saw yesterday.

(= This is the dog. + I saw the dog yesterday.)

Whose : **Shows possession (used for people or things).**

She is the girl *whose* dog ran away.

(= She is the girl. + Her dog ran away.)

Pattern Practice 1:

Fill in the blanks with the correct ***Relative Pronoun:*** *who, which, that, whose*

There may be more than one correct answer.

1. This is the chef __________ created the dish.
2. The structure __________ we visited yesterday is old.
3. The recipe, __________ uses red-pepper paste (고추장), is from Korea.
4. She is the architect __________ designed the landmark.
5. She is the girl ______________ bag is blue.
6. He is the tourist __________ asked about the building.
7. The dish ___________ you recommended was delicious.
8. The chef, _____________ restaurant is famous, uses the freshest ingredients.
9. The festival ___________ celebrates traditional foods is in December.
10. The skyscraper __________ we saw is the 63 building.

Grammar Focus 2: Omitting Relative Pronouns

In some cases, ***Relative Pronouns*** can be omitted when they are the ***object*** of the relative clause.

Example: The dish ***that we ate*** was spicy. → The dish ***we ate*** was spicy.

Pattern Practice 2:

Rewrite the sentences, omitting the ***Relative Pronoun***.

1. This is the recipe that I used.

____

2. The architect who we met was friendly.

____

3. The building which they built looks amazing.

____

4. The restaurant that he opened is popular.

____

5. The foods which you brought are delicious.

____

6. The person whom I saw at the museum was the guide.

____

7. The building that they visited is in Rome.

____

8. The herbs which she added gave it a strong flavor.

____

9. The book that I borrowed was about architecture.

____

10. The landmarks which we studied are historical.

____

Dialogue (Listening and Speaking):

Listen to the dialogue and fill in the missing words. Then practice the dialogue with your partner twice.

Anna:	Hi, Mark! Did you see the stall that has Moroccan (1) ____________?
Mark:	Yes! I tried the **tagine**, which is their (2) ____________ dish.
Anna:	I loved the (3) ____________ that they used. Have you seen the **stall** that shows famous (4) ________________?
Mark:	Not yet. Is it the one that has the model of the Eiffel Tower?
Anna:	Yes, and it also includes the Taj Mahal, which is beautifully **crafted**.
Mark:	That sounds amazing. Did you visit the Italian section that has pizza-making?
Anna:	I did! The chef, who was very friendly, shared his (5) ____________ with me.
Mark:	That's great. I want to try the sushi bar, which is near the entrance.
Anna:	Don't forget the dessert corner, which has ***baklava*** and other **treats**!

Key words: tagine 야채와 고기로 만든 북아프리카 스튜 요리 / stall 노점, 가판대 / crafted 공들여 만든 / baklava 중동 지역의 전통 디저트 / treat 간식, 특별한 음식

Dialogue questions: Write the answers to the dialogue questions, then ask and answer these questions with your partner.

1. What foods did Anna and Mark talk about?

____

2. What building models were displayed in the pavilion?

____

3. Who shared a recipe with Anna?

____

4. Where is the sushi bar located?

____

5. What desserts are in the dessert corner?

____

Conversation Practice: Ask and answer the following questions with your partner. Write your own answers first.

1. What Korean dish do you recommend that a foreigner try?

____

2. What's your favorite dessert or treat?

____

3. What's a landmark in Korea? Where is it?

____

4. Which restaurant that you visited last week has the best food?

____

5. What is something that you want to buy this weekend?

____

6. Do you have a friend who lives in another city? Who is he/she?

____

Reading: Read the following story. Write full sentence answers to the questions.

"Cultural Wonders Through Food and Architecture"

Ethnic foods and famous buildings often reflect the culture and history of a region. For example, the Great Wall of China, which is over 13,000 miles long, is a symbol of Chinese **ingenuity**. Similarly, dumplings (만두), which are a **staple** food in Chinese cuisine, represent the country's **diverse** flavors. They are very tasty, too!

The Colosseum, which was used for **gladiatorial** games in ancient Rome, is another **iconic** structure that tells stories of old **civilizations**. It's a landmark worth visiting.

Italian pizza, which originated in Naples, is **beloved** worldwide. Known for its thin crust, fresh ingredients, and simple toppings, pizza reflects the Italian love for quality and tradition. Each region of Italy has its own unique version on this classic dish, showcasing the country's culinary diversity.

Each dish, each building, has a story that connects people to their heritage. Food and architecture can serve as a bridge between the past and present, allowing people to experience the traditions and creativity of a culture.

Key words: ingenuity 독창성 / staple 주된, 주요한 / diverse 다양한 / gladiatorial 검투사의 / iconic 상징적인 / civilization 문명 / beloved 사랑받는

Reading Questions:

1. How long is the Great Wall of China?

____

2. What do Chinese dumplings represent?

____

3. Where did pizza originate?

____

4. What was the Colosseum used for in ancient Rome?

____

5. What do ethnic foods and famous buildings show about a region?

____

Editing: Write the correct *relative pronoun* in the sentence 

1. The dish *whose* we ate was delicious.

____

2. The building *who* was designed by the architect is a landmark.

____

3. The spices *who* she added made it delicious.

____

4. The landmark, *whose* we visited, is in Seoul.

____

5. The chef *which* cooked this meal is from Morocco.

____

Unit 11

Do you have your boarding pass ready?

Warm up: What's happening in the pictures? Make a sentence describing what is happening.

1. 

2. 

3. 

Picture 1: ______________________________

Picture 2: ______________________________

Picture 3: ______________________________

Vocabulary: Match each phrase with its correct meaning.

1. boarding pass	_____	**a.** a suitcase you carry onto the plane	
2. baggage claim area	_____	**b.** a card that shows your seat and flight details	
3. carry-on bag	_____	**c.** where you collect your checked luggage	
4. flight attendant	_____	**d.** a place where you have your belongings checked	
5. security checkpoint	_____	**e.** a person who helps passengers on the plane	
6. departure gate	_____	**f.** where you wait to board the plane	
7. check-in counter	_____	**g.** where you drop off luggage and get your pass	
8. customs officer	_____	**h.** a person who checks items brought into a country	
9. boarding time	_____	**i.** the time you need to get on the plane	
10. window seat	_____	**j.** a seat next to the airplane window	

Grammar Focus 1: Attributive nouns (속성명사, 형용사적 명사)

A noun (명사) is a person, place or a thing. An adjective (형용사) describes a noun. Sometime, a noun can act as an adjective. These are called ***Attributive Nouns.***

An ***Attributive Noun*** is a noun that acts like an adjective to describe another noun. It is usually placed before the main noun.

For example:

"**Boarding pass**" → The word ***boarding*** (a noun) describes the type of pass.

"**Departure gate**" → The word ***departure*** (a noun) describes the type of gate.

Rules to Remember:

1. The first noun describes the second noun.

   Example: *security checkpoint* → What kind of checkpoint? A **security** checkpoint.

2. The main noun is always the second word.

   Example: *baggage claim area* → The **area** is the main thing being described.

3. Attributive nouns are singular, even if they describe something plural.

   Example: *customs officer* (not **customs officers**, even though there may be more than one officer).

Pattern Practice 1A: Match the words to create **Attributive Nouns.**

1. passport _____
2. boarding _____
3. baggage _____
4. departure _____
5. carry-on _____
6. security _____
7. aisle _____

a. time
b. bag
c. claim area
d. seat
e. check
f. gate
g. officer

Pattern Practice 1B: Write the correct phrase from **Pattern Practice 1A** next to each definition.

1. The time your plane leaves: ____________
2. A person who checks your items: ____________
3. The seat at the end of a row: ____________
4. The place where you pick up your luggage: ____________
5. A small bag you take onto the plane: ____________
6. The gate where you wait to board your plane: ____________

Grammar Focus 2: Compound nouns (복합명사)

When an ***Attributive Noun*** combines with another noun, it can form a ***Compound Noun***.

A ***Compound Noun*** is a noun made up of two or more words that work together to name a single person, place, thing, or idea.

These words can be written as one word (e.g., *notebook*), as two separate words (e.g., *coffee table*), or with a hyphen (e.g., *mother-in-law*).

Compound Nouns make up many parts of speech. Look at the following box for a few examples.

Compound form	Example
Noun + Noun	Bathroom Airport
Noun + Verb	Haircut Snowfall
Noun + Adverb	Passerby Hanger-on
Verb + Adverb	Take-off Stopover
Adverb + Noun	Onlooker Bystander

Unit 11

Pattern Practice 2A: Fill in the blanks with the following compound nouns: 

baggage claim　carry on　passport control　boarding pass　take-off

1. Before getting on the plane, make sure you have your ________________. *(Noun + Noun)*
2. The pilot announced that we were ready for ________________. *(Noun + Adverb)*
3. After landing, we went to the ________________ to get our suitcases. *(Noun + Noun)*
4. You can only bring one ________________ bag onto the plane. *(Verb + Adverb)*
5. When traveling overseas, you need to go through ________________ to show your passport. *(Noun + Noun)*

Pattern Practice 2B: Read each statement and check if it is ***True*** or ***False***. 

1. In the compound noun "boarding pass", the word ***boarding*** describes the purpose of the pass. ***(True/False)***
2. In the compound noun "runway", the word ***run*** describes the type of plane. ***(True/False)***
3. In the compound noun "departure lounge", the word ***departure*** refers to the type of lounge where passengers wait before a flight. ***(True/False)***
4. In the compound noun "carry-on bag", the word ***bag*** describes the purpose of the carry-on. ***(True/False)***
5. In the compound noun "baggage claim", the word ***claim*** describes taking your luggage. ***(True/False)***

Dialogue (Listening and Speaking):

Listen to the dialogue and fill in the missing words. Then practice the dialogue with your partner twice.

Sarah: Do you have your (1) ____________________ ready?

John: Yes, I'm **all set**. I picked it up at the check-in counter.

Sarah: Great! Let's **head** to the (2) ____________________ now.

John: Good idea. I hope they let me take my carry-on bag without any **issue**.

Sarah: They should, as long as it's the right size.

John: Do you know what time the (3) ____________________ is?

Sarah: It's written on your pass. I think we're boarding at Gate 12, the departure gate.

John: Great. I hope I got a (4) ____________________.

Sarah: I prefer an aisle seat. Oh, and don't forget, we need to go through customs after we land.

John: Right, and we'll pick up our luggage at the (5) ____________________. I'm looking forward to having a **nap** on the plane. I'm tired. It was a long day. The airport was crowded with **onlookers** watching the music performance in the waiting area.

Key words: all set 준비가 된 / head ~로 향하다 / issue 문제 / nap 낮잠 / onlooker 구경하는 사람

Conversation Practice: Complete each question with one word to make a compound noun. Then ask the questions to your partner and write your partner's answer in the space below.

Remember to add an 's' to the verbs when using ***he, she,*** or ***it***.

1. Do you have a ______ port?
   (your partner's answer) ______________________________
2. How often do you fly on an ______ plane?
   (your partner's answer) ______________________________
3. What do you like to do at the ______ end?
   (your partner's answer) ______________________________
4. When did you last get a hair ______?
   (your partner's answer) ______________________________
5. What is one thing you put in your ______ ______ bag?
   ____

Reading: Read the following story. Write full sentence answers to the questions.

When you arrive at the airport, the first thing to do is to go to the check-in desk. Here, you can show your boarding pass and drop off your luggage. After that, you'll go through security where your bag will be checked. Once that's done, you can **unwind** in the departure lounge until it's time to board the plane. The flight attendants will help you find your seat on the plane. When the plane arrives at the destination, you can go to the baggage claim to pick up your bags.

As you wait in the lounge, you may see a **bystander** watching people, probably waiting for a friend or family member. Sometimes, you can see bystanders near the gate, hoping to get a **glimpse** of a **celebrity** or take a picture of them for their job.

Airports are full of many types of people. Some people may feel **jittery** being at an airport, especially if it's busy. Happy travels!

Key words: unwind 긴장을 풀다 / bystander 구경하는 사람 / glimpse 흘끗 봄 / celebrity 유명인 / jittery 초조한

Reading Questions:

1. What is the first thing you need to do when you arrive at the airport?

___

2. Where can you go to pick up your suitcase after the plane lands?

___

3. Who helps you find your seat and gives you instructions on the plane?

___

4. What might a bystander do at an airport?

___

5. Why might some people feel jittery at the airport?

___

Editing: Correct the errors in the following sentences. 

1. You can pick up your luggage at the baggage claims.

___

2. Before boarding, go to the check-ins desk to get your ticket.

___

3. The flight attendance gave us instructions about the emergency exits.

___

4. Please wait in the depart lounge until your flight is called.

___

5. The pilot announced that we were ready for take-offing.

___

Unit 11

Unit 12

Review

Unit 07: What do you want to do?

Vocabulary: Write the English meanings for the Korean words.

decide forget hope need plan want

1. 희망하다 ____________
2. 결정하다 ____________
3. 필요하다 ____________
4. 잊다 ____________
5. 계획하다 ____________
6. 원하다 ____________

Pattern Practice: Fill in the blanks using the correct ***Verb***.

~~would like~~ decided forgets hates hope needs plan

1. I _*would like*_ to visit Paris next summer.
2. She ____________ to eat spicy food because she sweats too much.
3. My friend ____________ to get a gym membership last week.
4. He ____________ to wake up at 8:00 AM to be on time for his 9 AM class.
5. My friends and I ____________ to go to the beach every weekend.

6. He ______________ to bring his book every week.

7. I ______________ we can be good friends.

Reading: Read the following story and answer the questions.

Let's Make Memories!

Hey there! Do you like to go to concerts? I sure do! Let me share our plans to **attend** a concert with my friends.

First, we all decided to go to a *BLACKPINK* concert. *BLACKPINK* is a group we all love, and we found out they're **performing** nearby.

Next, we needed to check the concert date and buy tickets online. We bought seats together, so we could enjoy the music as a group.

On the concert day, we'll meet up at my friend's house. We'll get ready together and choose cool **outfits** or even matching shirts!

Then, we'll go to the stadium. We'll grab some snacks and drinks and find our seats. When the music starts, we'll sing and dance along. It'll be so much fun, with lights flashing and everyone cheering.

After the concert, we'll talk about our favorite parts and have dinner together. It's all about **creating memories** and having an amazing time.

Key words: attend 참석하다 / performing 공연하다 / outfits 의상 / creating memories 추억 만들기

Reading Questions:

1. What did the group decide to do?

   a. watch a movie
   b. attend a concert
   c. go to a theme park
   d. have a picnic

2. How did they buy tickets for the concert?

   a. at the stadium
   b. from a friend
   c. online
   d. at a ticket booth

3. What will they do after the concert?

   a. go home and sleep
   b. talk about their favorite parts and have dinner
   c. go shopping and play games
   d. go to another concert

Unit 08: Do you enjoy being active?

Vocabulary: Write the English words for the Korean meanings.

avoid   enjoy   finish   keep   mind   quit   start

1. 신경 쓰다 ____________________
2. 유지하다 ____________________
3. 피하다 ____________________
4. 즐기다 ____________________
5. 시작하다 ____________________
6. 그만두다 ____________________
7. 끝내다 ____________________

Pattern Practice: Fill in the blanks using ***Infinitives*** or ***Gerunds***.

Example: They avoid _going_ (go) outside in the summers.

1. They enjoy ______________ *(play)* board games on weekends.
2. He plans ______________ *(start)* a new job next month.
3. She decided ______________ *(learn)* how to cook Italian cuisine.
4. We would like ______________ *(visit)* Japan during cherry blossom season.
5. They hate ______________ *(clean)* the house on Sundays.
6. I hope ______________ *(travel)* to Paris someday.
7. He forgot ____________________ *(pick up)* his dry cleaning from the store.
8. She loves ______________ *(read)* mystery novels before bed.

9. You should quit ______________ *(play)* games in class.

10. We don't mind ______________ *(watch)* reruns of our favorite TV show.

Dialogue: Practice the following dialogue and answer the questions.

Amy: Hey, Stephanie! Do you know about the new way to **lose weight**?

Stephanie: No, what is it?

Amy: It's singing and dancing! I read that it's a fun way to **lose extra kilograms.**

Stephanie: Really? How does it work?

Amy: Well, when you start singing and dancing, your body moves a lot. Singing keeps your energy up, and dancing makes you sweat and **burn calories.**

Stephanie: That sounds fun! I love singing and dancing.

Amy: Me too! It doesn't feel like exercising because you're having so much fun.

Stephanie: So, how often do you need to do it to lose weight?

Amy: They say that even just 30 minutes a day can make a difference. You can sing along to your favorite songs while dancing around your room.

Stephanie: I plan to try that! Thanks for telling me about it, Amy.

Amy: No problem, Stephanie. Let's start singing and dancing our way to a healthier lifestyle together.

Key words: lose weight 체중 감량하다 / lose extra kilograms 여분의 체중을 줄이다 / burn calories 칼로리를 태우다

Dialogue Questions:

1. What is the new way to lose weight?

   a. eating fruits and vegetables　　b. taking weight loss pills

   c. running on a treadmill　　d. singing and dancing

2. What keeps your energy up while singing and dancing?

   a. dancing　　b. both

   c. singing　　d. none of these

3. How often does Amy say you need to sing and dance to make a difference?

   a. 15 minutes a day　　b. 30 minutes a day

   c. 1 hour a day　　d. 2 hours a day

Unit 09: Have you planned your trip yet?

Vocabulary: Match the words to the definitions.

1. itinerary
   a. visiting famous places to learn about them
   b. a plan or schedule for a trip
   c. a place with many people at the same time
2. crowded
   a. a place filled with many people at the same time
   b. something that makes you feel calm and peaceful
   c. a timetable for a journey
3. relaxing
   a. visiting famous places to learn about them
   b. something that makes you feel calm and peaceful
   c. feeling very tired after doing something
4. exhausting
   a. feeling very tired after doing something
   b. feeling very happy after doing something
   c. a full schedule

Pattern Practice 1: Circle the ***Adjective*** and underline the ***Noun*** in the following sentences.

1. an exciting adventure
2. the exhausted tourist
3. The view is beautiful.
4. The tourists are happy.

Pattern Practice 2: Circle the correct ***Adjective*** ending.

1. The holiday was ***exhausting/exhausted***.
2. His vacation was ***satisfying/satisfied***.
3. Our trip was ***amazing/amazed***.
4. I hope to feel ***relaxing/relaxed*** on my holiday.

Reading: Read the following story and answer the questions.

Planning a trip can be exciting. First, you need an itinerary. This is a plan that shows where you will go and what you will do. For example, you can schedule time for visiting famous places, like museums, parks, or places of historic interest.

When you visit these places, they might be crowded. That means there are many people in one place. It can be noisy, but it is still interesting.

After a busy day, you may want to do something more relaxing, like sitting by the pool or reading.

Sometimes, trips can make you feel exhausted. This happens when you do too many things and don't rest enough. Remember to balance busy days with relaxing ones to enjoy your trip!

Reading Questions:

1. What is an itinerary?

____

2. Why might some places be crowded?

____

3. What is an example of something relaxing to do on a trip?

____

4. How can you avoid feeling exhausted on a trip?

____

Unit 10: This is the teacher *who* helps me.

Vocabulary: Match the words to the definitions.

1. **heritage**
   a. a tall building
   b. a region of a country
   c. something you inherit, like culture or traditions
2. **architect**
   a. a person who cooks food
   b. a person who designs buildings
   c. a person who writes books
3. **skyscraper**
   a. a big park
   b. a wide road
   c. a very tall building
4. **landmark**
   a. a famous place or building
   b. a type of animal
   c. a piece of furniture
5. **region**
   a. a large area of land
   b. a kind of car
   c. a small table

6. **ingenuity**

a. cleverness and creativity to solve problems

b. a place where people live

c. a type of game

7. **diverse**

a. The group has no people.

b. The people are all the same.

c. The people are from different places or backgrounds.

Pattern Practice 1: Fill in the blanks with the correct ***Relative Pronoun: who, which, that, whose***.

1. A chef is a person __________ cooks food.
2. Sushi is a Japanese dish __________ is made with rice and fish.
3. People __________ visit Paris often see the Eiffel Tower.
4. A tourist is someone __________ likes to explore new places.
5. A restaurant __________ serves traditional food is a wonderful place to learn about culture.
6. The man __________ backpack was full of souvenirs looked happy.
7. The market, __________ is close to my house, has many nice items.

Pattern Practice 2: Rewrite the sentences, omitting the ***Relative Pronoun***.

1. The food, which they cooked, looks tasty.

   ____

2. The textbook that he made is interesting.

   ____

3. The class that we took was too difficult.

   ____

Dialogue: Practice the dialogue and answer the questions.

Emma:	This is my first time in Italy! I'm so excited to try the pasta, which everyone says is delicious here.
Liam:	Me too! I love Italian cuisine, which is world famous.
Emma:	Do you know the name of the chef who made this pasta? It's so good.
Liam:	I don't, but this restaurant, whose sign says "Family-Owned", must be a famous one.
Emma:	I heard the Colosseum is a landmark that everyone should see.
Liam:	Yes, for sure. Rome is a city where history is everywhere. I also want to visit the Leaning Tower of Pisa. It's not a skyscraper, but it looks interesting.
Emma:	Nice! Italy has so many diverse regions to visit and enjoy.
Liam:	Let's take a picture in front of a landmark that we'll always remember.
Emma:	Sounds good! Get your camera ready.

Dialogue Questions:

1. What kind of cuisine do Emma and Liam talk about?

   ____

2. Who made the pasta that Emma likes?

   ____

3. What is the name of the landmark that Emma mentions first?

   ____

4. What does Liam say about Rome?

   ____

5. What does Emma say about Italy's regions?

   ____

Unit 11: Do you have your boarding pass ready?

Unit 12

Vocabulary: Write the Korean meanings for the English words.

1. boarding pass ________________
2. departure gate ________________
3. passport ________________
4. aisle ________________
5. carry-on bag ________________

Pattern Practice: Fill in the blanks with the correct words.

carry-on   aisle seat   boarding pass   passport control   window seat

1. You need to show your ________________ before you can go through security.
2. My small suitcase is a ________________, so I can take it on the plane with me.
3. At ________________, the security officer checked my ID and asked me a few questions.
4. I prefer sitting in an ________________ because I like to stretch my legs during the flight.
5. I love sitting in a ________________ so I can look outside during the flight.

Dialogue: Practice the dialogue and answer the questions.

> Anna: Hi, Ben! Are you ready for the flight?
>
> Ben: I think so. I have my carry-on bag, my passport, and my ticket.
>
> Anna: Good! Don't forget, we need to check the flight schedule on the departure board.
>
> Ben: Right. Do you know what time the plane takes off?
>
> Anna: Yes, it takes off at 10:30 a.m. But remember, we have a stopover in Chicago.
>
> Ben: A stopover? How long will we stay there?
>
> Anna: About two hours. Then we'll take the next flight to New York.
>
> Ben: I hope the waiting area at the Chicago airport isn't too crowded. I dislike being in crowded places.
>
> Anna: Me too. Oh, look! There's the flight attendant standing next to the customer service desk. Let's ask her if we're at the correct gate.
>
> Ben: Good idea! We should also double-check the boarding pass to be sure.
>
> Anna: Yes, better safe than sorry!

Dialogue Questions:

1. What does Ben have with him?

   ____

2. What time does the plane take off?

   ____

3. Where is the stopover?

   ____

4. How long is the stopover?

____

5. Who do Anna and Ben want to ask about the gate?

____

Editing: Correct the errors in the following sentences.

1. We got our *boarding paper* at the check-in counter.

____

2. The plane is leaving from the *depart door* soon.

____

3. After the flight landed, we went to the *arriving door.*

____

4. I like sitting in the *row seat* because it's easier to get up.

____

5. The *flight helper* gave us drinks during the flight.

____

Answer Key

Unit 01

Vocabulary:

1. c	**2.** i	**3.** a	**4.** j	**5.** b
6. d	**7.** f	**8.** e	**9.** h	**10.** g

Pattern Practice:

1. Who attended a lecture today?
2. What was the lecture about?
3. Where did the lecture take place?
4. When did the lecture start?
5. Why did David attend the lecture?
6. How did he take notes?
7. Who did he attend the lecture with? / With whom did he attend the lecture?

Dialogue:

1. Sports Festival	**2.** Which	**3.** Why
4. When	**5.** Which	**6.** Who

Reading Questions:

1. Because it is a simple act of kindness.
2. To prevent the spread of germs and show consideration for those around you.
3. I should keep my voice low in libraries or study areas.
4. They are “Thank you” and “I’m sorry.”
5. It helps create a positive environment and makes life more pleasant for everyone.

Exercises:

1. Who is in the photography club?
2. Where does the Sports Festival take place?
3. When will the Shingu Expo take place?
4. How do they enjoy campus events?
5. Why does Alex join college clubs?

Unit 02

Vocabulary:

1. e	2. g	3. j	4. i	5. a
6. h	7. b	8. f	9. d	10. c

Pattern Practice 1:

1. yourself	2. herself	3. themselves
4. myself	5. himself	6. themselves
7. itself	8. herself	9. itself
10. yourself		

Pattern Practice 2:

1. you	2. me	3. him	4. them	5. themselves
6. her	7. him	8. himself	9. us	10. you

Dialogue:

1. Saturday afternoon	2. jazz concert	3. myself
4. get tickets	5. ourselves	6. ourselves

Reading Questions:

1. She gained weight because she needed to bulk up for her role in the movie.
2. She eats six eggs and lots of bacon.
3. She challenges herself by eating two hamburgers at a fast-food restaurant, finishing every bite.
4. She must make herself stumble onto the floor.
5. She feels very proud of herself for having completed her role.

Editing:

1. The young man broke a glass and cut himself very badly.
2. The girl hurt herself while playing baseball.
3. Can you help me with the assignment?
4. She trusted herself to deal with the situation.
5. I saw him at the library last week.

Sentence Scramble:

1. Sue and Frank booked the concert tickets by themselves.
2. She made the cake by herself.
3. My friend talks to himself when he's nervous.
4. The children enjoyed themselves at the amusement park.
5. The students should take care of themselves when they feel stressed.

Unit 03

Vocabulary:

1. h	2. b	3. d	4. j	5. g
6. f	7. c	8. a	9. e	10. i

Pattern Practice:

1. She enjoys learning about climate change.
2. My friends like to discuss the ecosystem.
3. You need to recycle to reduce pollution.
4. Sujin studies reforestation every day.
5. Many animals struggle to survive due to wildfires.
6. The children learn about renewable energy at school.
7. I am researching climate change now.
8. My brother cares about recycling paper.
9. It causes a lot of wildfires in the summer.
10. They usually talk about the greenhouse effect.
11. The student understands the importance of conservation.
12. We are planning to discuss climate change next month.
13. Jack has an assignment related to renewable energy.
14. He is focusing on sustainability in his studies.
15. Wildfires spread quickly in natural areas.

Dialogue:

1. heatwaves
2. climate change
3. destroyed
4. energy-efficient
5. reforestation

Reading Questions:

1. It is the rise in greenhouse gases like CO2 and methane, which lead to global warming.
2. It makes the water more acidic, harming marine life and ecosystems.
3. It means meeting our needs today without harming the future.
4. We can support sustainability by recycling.
5. It can help reduce our reliance on fossil fuels.

Editing:

1. She enjoys joining clean-up activities on weekends.
2. My friend has a solar-powered car.
3. They were excited about the environmental project.
4. He does research on renewable energy every evening.
5. We like to learn about climate change.

Sentence Scramble:

1. The recycling bins are full.
2. Jenny participated in planting trees.
3. The bird sings in the forest.
4. The students join clean-up events every summer.
5. My sister enjoys recycling paper with her friends.

Unit 04

Vocabulary:

1. a	**2.** a	**3.** b	**4.** b	**5.** a
6. b	**7.** a	**8.** a	**9.** a	**10.** a

Pattern Practice:

1. The girls look very happy to go skating.
2. The sky looks blue.
3. I don't feel so good today.
4. She is my classmate.
5. The chicken soup smells delicious.
6. They are college students.
7. The movie seems interesting.
8. The children are excited about the trip.

9. Your idea <u>sounds</u> great.
10. Sumi <u>feels</u> tired after the workout.

Dialogue:

1. sleep in
2. boiled eggs
3. eat out
4. wash my face
5. put on
6. get dressed
7. meet up with
8. surf the internet

Reading Questions:

1. They commute to campus using public transport, bikes, or by walking.
2. They usually take their lunch break at campus cafés.
3. They bring lunchboxes with a variety of food, such as sandwiches, fried rice, stir-fried noodles, or salads.
4. They spend their afternoons attending additional classes, participating in study groups, or working on assignments.
5. They balance part-time jobs, sports, and socializing at pubs or beaches in their spare time.

Editing:

1. He <u>looks</u> happy after the meeting.
2. The weather <u>is</u> nice today.
3. The flowers <u>smell</u> wonderful in the garden.
4. The apple pie <u>tastes</u> delicious.
5. My sister <u>was</u> excited about her holidays.

Sentence Scramble:

1. The weather seems perfect for a picnic.
2. She became a famous writer.
3. The sky appears cloudy today.
4. My friend looks happy with the new job.
5. I feel tired after the long day.

Unit 05

Vocabulary:

1. c	2. d	3. f	4. g	5. a
6. i	7. j	8. e	9. b	10. h

Pattern Practice:

• Complete the sentences with ***many*** or ***much***.

1. There are many people at the Christmas concert.
2. We drank too much coffee at the meeting.
3. I saw many birds flying over the lake.
4. Don't feel much pressure to succeed.
5. There isn't much sugar left in the jar.

• Complete the sentences with ***a few*** / ***few*** or ***a little*** / ***little***.

1. I need a few minutes to think about it.
2. Lynn liked sweet coffee, so she added a little sugar to her tea.
3. Minsu made a few mistakes during the presentation, but it was good.
4. Sarah feels sad because she has few friends who understand her well.
5. He had little chance of winning the tennis match, but he did his best.

Dialogue:

1. influential
2. a lot of
3. lots of
4. much
5. effective
6. entertainment

Reading Questions:

1. K-culture refers to cultural elements from South Korea.
2. *Squid Game* and *My Love from the Star* are mentioned.
3. It is a popular South Korean television variety show.
4. They turn on the subtitles while watching.
5. Korean beauty products and traditional dishes like *bulgogi, kimchi,* and *bibimbap* are gaining popularity.

Editing:

1. A few/Many people like to travel during the holidays.
2. She drank too much water after hiking.
3. The professor encouraged the students to ask many questions, but they asked few questions during the lecture.
4. How much flour do you need?
5. I tried to find information about the topic, but I couldn't find much information about that topic online.

Sentence Scramble:

1. We ate lots of pizza at the party.
2. How many people are there in the meeting room?
3. She doesn't have much time to finish her homework.
4. There is little water in the bottle.
5. He feels a lot of pressure to finish his work.

Unit 06

Unit 01:

Vocabulary:

1. syllabus
2. semester
3. sports festival
4. career fair
5. midterms
6. final exam
7. extracurricular activities
8. student union
9. club fair
10. meals at the college cafeteria

Grammar:

1. What is she doing?
2. Where did you buy this?
3. When does your class begin?
4. How did you come here?
5. Why did you want to go (there)?

Unit 02:

Vocabulary:

1. play
2. theater
3. applause
4. performance
5. pop culture
6. orchestra
7. exhibition
8. audience
9. conductor
10. celebrity

Grammar:

1. No one praised Sumi for finishing her project, but Sumi is proud of herself.
2. We have to serve ourselves at the buffet.
3. He always plays computer games by himself.
4. Because there was no host, the presenters introduced themselves to the group.
5. Jenny went on a trip alone, and she found herself lost in the new city.
6. I will meet you at the top of the mountain.
7. He showed her the way to the museum.
8. The secretary told him about the meeting time.
9. My friend likes to tell me the story of his travels.
10. May I ask you a question?

Unit 03:

Vocabulary:

1. recycling
2. greenhouse gases
3. wildfires
4. conservation
5. ecosystem
6. reforestation
7. sustainability
8. climate change
9. pollution
10. renewable energy

Grammar:

1. Pollution harms animals and plants.
2. Trees give us oxygen to breathe.
3. Wildfires spread quickly in dry forests.
4. Climate change makes weather more extreme.
5. Factories produce a lot of greenhouse gases.
6. The community cleans the park every weekend.
7. Water pollution affects fish and other sea life.

8. Everyone needs to help the environment.

9. Plastic bags cause problems for wildlife.

10. Recycling saves resources and energy.

Unit 04:

Vocabulary:

1.	get dressed	2.	eat out
3.	surf the Internet	4.	bring a lunch box
5.	commute	6.	sleep in
7.	go to class	8.	hang out
9.	put on makeup	10.	wash one's face

Grammar:

1. We are/were/weren't/felt/seemed tired after the long trip.
2. This soup tastes sour.
3. The weather was perfect for a picnic yesterday.
4. My dog is very friendly even to strangers.
5. They were late for the meeting last week.
6. Kate looks happy after the good news.
7. The flowers smell good in the garden.
8. The child is/feels sleepy after playing soccer.
9. His explanation is clear and concise.
10. She is excited about her trip to Africa.

Unit 05:

Vocabulary:

1. attention
2. memorable
3. popularity
4. global spread
5. cuisine
6. influence
7. skincare
8. beauty products
9. Korean wave
10. entertainment

Grammar:

1. Anne bought many apples at the supermarket.
2. We don't have much time to finish this task.
3. Minsu has many friends in his class.
4. I ate too much cake at the party.
5. He has much homework to do this weekend.
6. We have a little free time this afternoon.
7. Jack has a little money left in his wallet.
8. There are a few eggs left in the refrigerator.
9. Some students need a little help with their assignment.
10. There are a few chairs in the meeting room.

Unit 07

Vocabulary:

1. f	2. g	3. b	4. d	5. a
6. e	7. c	8. j	9. h	10. i

Pattern Practice 1:

1. I want to eat pizza for dinner tonight.
2. She loves to go to the beach on the weekends.
3. We need to buy groceries for the week.
4. He will try to learn Spanish before his trip to Mexico.
5. They plan to visit their grandparents next month.
6. She decided to study medicine in college.
7. I hope to travel to Japan someday.
8. He hates to sleep after eating a big meal.
9. She would like to learn how to play the guitar.
10. We like to clean the house before guests arrive.

Pattern Practice 2:

1. want 2. hope 3. plan 4. likes

Pattern Practice 3:

1. I want to buy a new car.
2. He needs to go home.
3. I would like to eat fried chicken for dinner.
4. BTS hopes to meet many fans.
5. My friends and I decided to go to the beach.

Dialogue:

1. want to get 2. decided to start 3. promise to be
4. hope to visit 5. forget to have

Reading Questions:

1. They want to make their neighborhoods cleaner and more attractive.
2. They plan to play with the animals, feed them, and keep the animals safe and happy.
3. Because they can be lonely.
4. We need to remember that our elders have wisdom to share.

Editing:

1. She wants to go to the store after school.
2. He needs to study more for the exam tomorrow.
3. I try to learn Japanese on the weekends.
4. We hope to go camping this summer.
5. They would like to travel around the world someday.

Writing Time:

Answers will vary

Unit 08

Vocabulary:

1. e	2. d	3. f	4. a	5. g
6. c	7. b	8. j	9. h	10. i

Pattern Practice 1:

1. I enjoy reading books in my free time.
2. He finishes practicing the piano.
3. They hate eating with dirty hands.
4. She quit working at her job last week.
5. I avoid waking up early on the weekends.

Pattern Practice 2:

1. She needs to study for the test tonight.
2. When I finish writing this letter, I'll help you.
3. I want to buy a new laptop soon.
4. He quit smoking and feels much better now.
5. We forgot to bring our books to school.
6. They decided to travel to Europe this summer.
7. She avoids walking in the rain.
8. You need to practice more grammar.
9. I love to go/going to the mountains.
10. I don't mind watching scary movies.

Dialogue:

1. enjoy playing
2. start running
3. avoid feeling
4. quit making
5. keep pushing

Reading Questions:

1. She wants to be healthy.
2. She starts stretching to warm up her muscles.
3. She enjoys doing yoga.
4. Yoga helps her relax and stay flexible.
5. Cathy plans to go for a walk with her dog.

Editing:

1. He wants to learn how to play soccer.
2. Sarah loves to dance and sing in the band.
3. We need to buy some groceries for the week.
4. He hates to wake up early in the morning.
5. They avoid doing their projects.

Writing Time:

Answers will vary

Unit 09

Vocabulary:

1. c 2. a 3. g 4. e 5. i
6. h 7. b 8. j 9. d 10. f

Pattern Practice 1:

1. breathtaking 2. crowded 3. relaxing
4. exciting 5. dirty 6. full
7. happy 8. small 9. unhappy
10. large

Pattern Practice 2:

1. exhausted 2. boring 3. interesting
4. relaxed 5. exciting 6. satisfying
7. disappointed 8. fascinating 9. confused
10. amazed

Dialogue:

1. hiking
2. exhausting
3. prepared
4. itinerary
5. memorable

Reading Questions:

1. She had always wanted to visit Tokyo.
2. She found it exhilarating.
3. Mount Fuji and the Golden Pavilion.
4. It is a traditional Japanese hot spring.
5. She felt exhausted but happy.

Editing:

1. tiring / The journey was <u>tiring</u>.
2. relaxing / The resort is very <u>relaxing</u>.
3. interested / I am <u>interested</u> in visiting Italy.
4. boring / The beach was so <u>boring</u> that we left early.
5. exhausting / The sightseeing tour was <u>exhausting</u>.

Unit 10

Vocabulary:

1. b
2. f
3. e
4. c
5. g
6. j
7. h
8. a
9. d
10. i

Pattern Practice 1:

1. who/that
2. that
3. which
4. who/that
5. whose
6. who/that
7. that
8. whose
9. that
10. that

Pattern Practice 2:

1. This is the recipe I used.
2. The architect we met was friendly.
3. The building they made looks amazing.
4. The restaurant he opened is popular.
5. The foods you brought are delicious.
6. The person I saw at the museum was the guide.
7. The building they visited is in Rome.
8. The herbs she added gave it a strong flavor.
9. The book I borrowed was about architecture.
10. The landmarks we studied are historical.

Dialogue:

1. cuisine
2. traditional
3. spices
4. landmarks
5. recipe

Dialogue Questions:

1. Moroccan cuisine, tagine, pizza, sushi, baklava.
2. Eiffel Tower, Taj Mahal.
3. An Italian chef.
4. Near the entrance.
5. Baklava and other desserts.

Reading Questions:

1. It is over 13,000 miles long.
2. It represents the country's diverse flavors.
3. It originated in Naples, Italy.

4. It was used for gladiatorial games.
5. They show the culture and history of a region.

Editing:

1. The dish that we ate was delicious.
2. The building that was designed by the architect is a landmark.
3. The spices that she added made it delicious.
4. The landmark, which we visited, is in Seoul.
5. The chef who/that cooked this meal is from Morocco.

Unit 11

Vocabulary:

1. b	2. c	3. a	4. e	5. d
6. f	7. g	8. h	9. i	10. j

Pattern Practice 1A:

1. e	2. a	3. c	4. f	5. b
6. g	7. d			

Pattern Practice 1B:

1. boarding time	2. security officer	3. aisle seat
4. baggage claim area	5. carry-on bag	6. departure gate

Pattern Practice 2A:

1. boarding pass	2. take-off	3. baggage claims
4. carry on	5. passport control	

Pattern Practice 2B:

1. True 2. False 3. True 4. False 5. True

Dialogue:

1. boarding pass
2. security checkpoint
3. boarding time
4. window seat
5. baggage claim area

Conversation Practice:

1. passport
2. airplane
3. weekend
4. haircut
5. carry-on bag

Reading Questions:

1. The first thing to do is to go to the check-in desk.
2. You can go to the baggage claim.
3. The flight attendants will help.
4. You may see a bystander watching people, probably waiting for a friend or family member. Sometimes, you can see bystanders near the gate, hoping to get a glimpse of a celebrity or take a picture of them for their job.
5. The airport might be busy.

Editing:

1. You can pick up your luggage at the baggage **claim**.
2. Before boarding, go to the check-**in** desk to get your ticket.
3. The flight **attendant** gave us instructions about the emergency exits.
4. Please wait in the **departure** lounge until your flight is called.
5. The pilot announced that we were ready for take-**off**.

Unit 12

Unit 07:

Vocabulary:

1. hope
2. decide
3. need
4. forget
5. plan
6. want
7. would like

Pattern Practice:

1. would like
2. hates
3. decided
4. needs
5. plan
6. forgets
7. hope

Reading Questions:

1. b
2. c
3. b

Unit 08:

Vocabulary:

1. mind
2. keep
3. avoid
4. enjoy
5. start
6. quit
7. finish

Pattern Practice:

1. playing
2. to start
3. to learn
4. to visit
5. to clean/cleaning
6. to travel
7. to pick up
8. to read/reading
9. playing
10. watching

Dialogue Questions:

1. d 2. c 3. b

Unit 09:

Vocabulary:

1. b 2. a 3. b 4. a

Pattern Practice 1:

1. An (exciting) adventure
2. The (exhausted) tourist
3. The view is (beautiful)
4. The tourists are (happy)

Pattern Practice 2:

1. exhausting 2. satisfying 3. amazing 4. relaxed

Reading Questions:

1. It is a plan that shows where you will go and what you will do.
2. There are many people in one place.
3. Sitting by the pool or reading.
4. By resting enough/by balancing busy days with relaxing ones.

Unit 10:

Vocabulary:

1. c 2. b 3. c 4. a 5. a
6. a 7. c

Pattern Practice 1:

1. who 2. that 3. who 4. who 5. that
6. whose 7. which

*Tip: Although you can use *that* to talk about people, it is better to use *who*: A chef is a person *that* cooks food. A chef is a person *who* cooks food.

That and *which* can often be used interchangeably, and the rules are different in American English and British English. To make it easier to understand, use *which* separated by commas. The book *that* I read was great. The book, *which* I read in one day, was great.

Pattern Practice 2:

1. The food they cooked looks tasty.
2. The textbook he made is interesting.
3. The class we took was too difficult.

Dialogue Questions:

1. They talk about Italian cuisine.
2. The chef made the pasta.
3. The landmark she mentions first is the Colosseum.
4. Rome is a city where history is everywhere.
5. Italy has so many diverse regions to visit and enjoy.

Unit 11:

Vocabulary:

1. boarding pass – 탑승권
2. departure gate – 출발 게이트
3. passport – 여권
4. aisle – 통로
5. carry-on bag – 기내 가방

Pattern Practice:

1. boarding pass
2. carry-on
3. passport control
4. aisle seat
5. window seat

Dialogue Questions :

1. He has his carry-on bag, passport, and ticket.
2. It takes off at 10.30 am.
3. It stops over in Chicago.
4. It is about 2 hours.
5. They want to ask the flight attendant.

Editing:

1. We got our *boarding pass* at the check-in counter.
2. The plane is leaving from the *departure gate* soon.
3. After the flight landed, we went to the *arrival gate*.
4. I like sitting in the *aisle seat* because it's easier to get up.
5. The *flight attendant* gave us drinks during the flight.

Workbook

Unit 01 : How's college life going?

Make questions using the following words (*who, when, where, what, why*) to match the given answers.

1. ______________________________? (what)
   He is reading a book.
2. ______________________________? (where/did)
   They traveled to France last summer.
3. ______________________________? (when/will)
   The meeting will start at 9 AM.
4. ______________________________? (what/does)
   She cooks dinner for the family.
5. ______________________________? (where/did)
   I went to the park with my friends.

Unit 02 : Are you going to enjoy yourself this weekend?

Complete the following sentences with the correct *Reflexive Pronouns*.

1. Jane hurt ______________ while exercising at the gym.
2. He looked at ______________ in the mirror and laughed.
3. The girls enjoyed ______________ at the playground.
4. My cat washed ______________after playing in the garden.
5. We enjoyed ______________ on the trip last weekend.
6. Andrew promised to finish the work by ______________.
7. We must take care of ______________ while using sharp tools.
8. They congratulated ______________ after winning the first prize.

9. James was proud of ________________ when finishing his project.

10. I enjoyed ________________ at the beach all day.

Unit 03: Did you watch the news about the heatwaves?

Complete the following sentences with the correct *Subject-Verb Agreement* form.

1. The Earth ________________ protection from pollution. (need)
2. The boys ________________ soccer after school. (play)
3. Conservation ________________ endangered animals. (protect)
4. Wildfires ________________ wide areas of forests every year. (destroy)
5. The birds usually ________________ in the morning. (sing)
6. The Earth's temperature ________________ due to global warming. (rise)
7. People ________________ away much trash. (throw)
8. Those cars ________________ the air with smoke. (pollute)
9. His teacher ________________ the lesson clearly. (explain)
10. My sister ________________ to music every evening. (listen)

Unit 04 : What's your daily routine?

Fill in the blanks with the correct *Linking Verb* to complete the sentence.

1. The students ________________ very excited about the sports festival.
2. The flowers ________________ fresh and fragrant.
3. Their hands ________________ cold after making a snowman.
4. John ________________ nervous before the interview.

5. The puppies ________________ very playful in the park.

6. We ________________ exhausted after running the full marathon.

7. The cake ________________ delicious. Everyone loved it.

8. The weather ________________ great when we were in Europe.

9. Your dress ________________ nice. I like it.

10. This milk ________________ spoiled. you shouldn't drink it.

Unit 05 : Have you heard of K-culture?

Complete the following sentences with *few* or *little*.

1. I have ________________ friends in this city.

2. My friend has ________________ money to buy a new car.

3. The guests have ________________ options for dinner tonight.

4. The tourists saw ________________ animals during the hike.

5. The students have ________________ free time on weekends because of their exams.

6. There are ________________ onions left in the grocery store.

7. They have ________________ patience for rude behavior.

8. Sumi added ________________ sugar to the coffee.

9. He has ________________ knowledge of his task.

10. There are ________________ students attending the seminar.

Unit 07: What do you want to do?

Vocabulary: Write the ***Verbs*** in English.

1. 원하다 ____________________
2. 필요하다 ____________________
3. 좋아하다 ____________________
4. 잊다 ____________________
5. 계획하다 ____________________
6. 희망하다 ____________________
7. 사랑하다 ____________________
8. 싫어하다 ____________________
9. 결정하다 ____________________

Pattern Practice: Underline the ***Verb*** and circle the ***Infinitive***.

Example: The boys _like_ (to eat) ice cream in the summer.

1. They need to finish their homework before watching TV.
2. He wants to buy a new car next year.
3. She loves to read books in her free time.
4. We hope to visit Paris during the summer vacation.
5. They plan to go hiking in the mountains this weekend.
6. I decided to take up painting as a hobby.
7. She would like to find a new job soon.
8. They forgot to save the file on the computer.

Editing: Find and correct the **errors** in the sentences.

1. He want to get a new job. ______________________________
2. I want to getting a driving license. ______________________________
3. I hope to getting an A grade in school. ______________________________
4. She needs to studying. ______________________________
5. We would like to going home. ______________________________

Unit 08: Do you enjoy being active?

Vocabulary: Write the ***verbs*** in English.

1. 피하다 ____________________
2. 시작하다 ____________________
3. 그만두다 ____________________
4. 유지하다 ____________________
5. 신경 쓰다 ____________________
6. 끝내다 ____________________
7. 즐기다 ____________________

Pattern Practice: Write the ***infinitive*** form or the ***gerund*** form.

Example: They start studying (study) after they practice basketball.

1. He would like ______________ *(try)* out for the school basketball team.
2. They decided ______________ *(travel)* to Europe for their summer vacation.
3. I started ______________ *(learn)* how to play the piano last month.
4. She hates ______________ *(cook)* dinner after a long day at work.
5. We need ______________ *(find)* a new apartment before the end of the month.

6. He enjoys _______________ *(play)* the guitar in his free time.

7. They plan __________________ *(go)* on a road trip next weekend.

8. He finished __________________ *(read)* the entire book in one sitting.

9. She loves __________________ *(read)* mystery novels before bedtime.

10. We dislike _______________ *(wait)* in long lines at the grocery store.

11. She keeps _______________ *(forget)* her keys in the taxi.

12. She wants _______________ *(visit)* all the famous landmarks in Europe.

13. I hope _______________ *(find)* a job that I truly enjoy.

Editing: Find and correct the **errors** in the sentences.

1. I enjoy to study. ________________________________

2. He enjoy listening to music. ________________________________

3. I love to listening to music. ________________________________

4. I quit to smoking. ________________________________

5. She likes to playing tennis. ________________________________

Unit 09: Have you planned your trip yet?

Vocabulary: Write the **meaning** of these words in Korean.

1. Destination	_______________	2. Itinerary	_______________
3. Bucket list	_______________	4. Reservation	_______________
5. Breathtaking	_______________	6. Noun	_______________
7. Adjective	_______________	8. Memorable	_______________
9. Exhausting	_______________	10. Resort	_______________

Pattern Practice 1: Underline the ***Noun*** and circle the ***Adjective*** in the following sentences.

1. The busy man travelled.
2. The students are busy.
3. John has a full itinerary.
4. Travel is rewarding.
5. The job was exhausting.

Pattern Practice 2: Choose the correct ***Adjective*** ending to complete the sentence.

1. His job is very ***interesting/interested***.
2. I enjoy hiking, it is ***exciting/excited***.
3. The mountain views were ***exhilarating/exhilarated***.
4. I was ***exhilarated/exhilarating*** by the views.

Editing: Find and correct the **errors** in the following sentences.

1. My vacation has exciting. ______________________________
2. My itinerary is excited. ______________________________
3. My work is tired today. ______________________________
4. Traveling can be so rewarded. ______________________________
5. The man are happy. ______________________________

Unit 10: This is the teacher *who* helps me.

Vocabulary: Write the meaning of the words in Korean.

1. Cuisine ____________________
2. Skyscraper ____________________
3. Iconic ____________________
4. Landmark ____________________
5. Diverse ____________________

Pattern Practice 1: Fill in the blanks with the correct ***relative pronoun***: ***who, which, that,*** or ***whose***.

1. A chef is someone ___________ cooks food.
2. This is the dish ___________ I ate in France last year.
3. A tourist is a person ___________ likes to visit new places.
4. *Gimbap* (김밥), ___________ is from Korea, is made with rice.
5. A waiter is a person ___________ serves food in a restaurant.
6. A region, ___________ has diverse cultures, is always interesting to visit.
7. This is the bag ___________ I bought during my trip to Thailand.
8. Do you know the man ___________ suitcase is next to the door?

Pattern Practice 2: Rewrite the sentences, omitting the ***Relative Pronoun***. If the ***Relative Pronoun*** can't be omitted, don't change the sentence.

1. This is the restaurant that we visited.

   ____

2. The pasta, which she made, was delicious.

   ____

3. I know a chef who cooks Italian food.

   ____

4. This is the region whose cuisine is famous.

   ____

5. The landmarks that tourists love to visit are beautiful.

   ____

Unit 11: Do you have your boarding pass ready?

Pattern Practice 1: Match the words to create ***Attributive Nouns***.

1. Boarding _____	a. checkpoint
2. Departure _____	b. pass
3. Baggage _____	c. gate
4. Carry-on _____	d. claim
5. Security _____	e. bag

Pattern Practice 2: Fill in the blanks with the correct words.

carry on　　take-off　　boarding pass
passport control　　flight attendant　　baggage claim

1. After landing, we went to ________________ to pick up our suitcases.
2. Make sure your ________________ fits in the overhead bin before boarding the plane.
3. Before going to the gate, we showed our documents at ________________.
4. The ________________ has your seat number and boarding time on it.
5. During ________________, the ________________ asked everyone to fasten their seat belts.

Editing: Find and correct the **errors** in the following sentences.

1. You need to show your boarding past before entering the gate.

____

2. I forgot my carry in bag at the gate.

____

3. We went to bagging claim to get our suitcases after the flight.

____

4. At passport check, they asked to see my visa.

____

5. The flight attended helped me with my seatbelt.

____

Campus English 103

Authors: **English Textbook Committee**
Giles Fordham
Jieun Hwang
Yoon-Jeong Hwang

Publisher: Shingu Publishing Co.

Design: eundesign

ISBN: 978-89-7668-287-1 03740

February 2026 Printing

Published by Shingu Publishing Co.
377, Gwangmyeong-ro, Jungwon-gu, Seongnam-si
Gyeonggi-do, South Korea
Tel. 031-741-3055